CHILDREN OF POVERTY

Studies on the Effects of Single Parenthood, the Feminization of Poverty, and Homelessness

edited by

STUART BRUCHEY
University of Maine

A GARLAND SERIES

ATTITUDES OF CHILDREN TOWARD THEIR HOMELESS PEERS

LAWRENCE C. GIBEL

GARLAND PUBLISHING, Inc.
NEW YORK & LONDON / 1996

Library of Congress Cataloging-in-Publication Data

Gibel, Lawrence C., 1946–
 Attitudes of children toward their homeless peers / Lawrence
C. Gibel.
  p. cm. — (Children of poverty)
 Includes bibliographical references and index.
 ISBN 0-8153-2539-8 (alk. paper)
 1. Homeless children—United States—Attitudes. 2. Home-
less students—United States—Public opinion. 3. Public opinion—
United States. 4. Children—United States—Attitudes. I. Title.
II. Series.
HV4505.G49 1996
305.23—dc20   96-36707

Printed on acid-free, 250-year-life paper
Manufactured in the United States of America

I dedicate this project to all the homeless children and their families. You seem to have been forgotten by the system but hopefully things will change, and people will change, and the world will be a better place to raise children.

I would also like to thank Hofstra University and especially Dr. Norweeta Milburn for all the contributions she made to the project. Without her it would not have been possible.

I would also like to thank the school district in which the study was run. I am indebted to the administrators, teachers and especially the students who took the time to participate and answer my questions. I wish I could thank each of you by name.

Finally, I want to express my appreciation to my fiance Joyce who helped in ways only she understands, my children Greg and Jessica who are so important to me and Joyce's boys, Scott and Brian who let me use the computer for a few minutes.

Contents

Tables

Figures

Appendices

Attitudes of Children Toward Their Homeless Peers

I
Review Of The Literature

Introduction

This study investigates whether housed children hold negative stereotypical ideas about their homeless peers. The study will also try to determine whether these stereotypes are generated by the label "homeless," the characteristics of being homeless such as poverty, or whether these stereotypes are held in response to an underlying racial prejudice.

As poverty increases due to a widening recession and increased unemployment, and affordable housing declines, homelessness is becoming an ever more important problem in the United States. This review will define homelessness and show that homeless children and their families are the fastest growing segment of the homeless population. It will also show how this population presents some of the country's most pressing problems (e.g., U. S. Department of Education, 1989). Homeless children are at slightly greater risk than poor children and at much greater risk than the general population for developmental delays, health problems and psychological problems, and to do poorly in school (Rafferty & Shinn, 1991).

Homeless children have poor attendance at school, do poorly when they attend school and are at high risk for dropping out before they complete high school (e.g., Rafferty & Rollins, 1989a). Many studies (e.g., Doolan, Georgedes, Dillman, & Willis, 1989; Eddowes & Hranitz, 1989) associate these school related problems with problems that result from being homeless. These include such things as poor medical care, an unstable home environment, the lack of funds to purchase school supplies or appropriate clothes, no quiet place to study, the transient nature of being homeless and moving from shelter to shelter.

Homeless children also have socialization difficulties in school. Some of these problems are suggested by theories such as Maslow's Hierarchy of Needs (Eddowes & Hranitz, 1989), Straub's devaluation theory (1996) and a process called "shelterization" described by Grunberg and Eagle (1990). In addition there are factors that may be involved in their socialization difficulties. These factors are suggested by research on attitudes toward individuals who are perceived to be different, such as disabled people, people from a different ethnic/racial group, etc. (e.g., Yuker, 1987; Sherman, 1990). For example, the children in school may have less positive attitudes toward homeless school children that may make them feel unwelcomed in school. In addition, the children in school may not want to be friends with children who are homeless. These attitudes may be attributable to their homelessness.

Moreover, homeless children are generally from poor families and a large percentage of their families are also ethnic minorities, the largest group of whom is Black. Other children in school may have prejudices toward homeless children that cannot be attributed to homelessness per se, but can be attributed to their negative attitudes toward poor people or minority people (e.g., McCombs & Gay, 1988).

Definition and Causes of Homelessness

The Stewart B. McKinney Act (P.L. 100-77, 1987) defines a homeless person as an individual who "lacks a fixed, regular and adequate residence" or has "a primary nighttime residence in a supervised publicly or privately operated shelter for temporary accommodations" (sect. 103(a)(1)(2)). The Congress of the United States (1988) felt that time limits, like the commonly used 30 day limit, were unrealistic because of the large number of families who have needed assistance beyond the 30 day limit. Some researchers have expanded the time limits of their definitions of homelessness to include having no shelter or limited shelter for any length of time (e.g., First, Toomey, & Rife, 1990).

Being homeless includes living in cheap hotels or motels, shelters run by religious organizations or public agencies, staying with family or friends, staying in places where no rent is paid (abandoned buildings) or places that do not qualify as a house such as cars, sheds, or shantys (First, Toomey, & Rife, 1990). For children and youth, the New Jersey Administrative Code (1990) expands this definition to include living in transitional or halfway houses for families or the mentally ill, an institution, a domestic violence or runaway shelter, or a home for adolescent mothers; residing in a hospital when one would have been released if one had a permanent residence; or being the child of a migrant family who lacks adequate housing.

Many researchers believe that homelessness is caused by the disappearance or unavailability of low income housing through gentrification, urban renewal, decay, fire, and eviction (Hartman, 1989; Mills & Ota, 1989). Bassuk (1984) noted that the number of rental units that cost 30 percent of income or less, fell by 70 percent between 1970 and 1980 from 5.1 to 1.2 million. There has also been an 80 percent cut in federally assisted housing for low income and special needs groups since 1981 (Carling, 1990). These cuts in housing have been compounded by inflation, the recession, increased unemployment, underemployment, and cuts in other federal and state programs targeted at the poor (Baxter & Hopper, 1981; Bassuk, 1984; Hopper, 1984; Hombs & Snyder, 1986; Grant, 1990; Kass & Silver, 1990; Stronge & Tenhouse, 1990). The presence or absence of family supports and social supports have been found to be contributing factors as well (Solarz & Bogat, 1990). Although estimates on the number of homeless people vary widely, there are currently more Americans homeless than at any time since the Great Depression (Bassuk, 1984; Rossi, 1990). The U.S. Department of Housing and Urban Development estimated that there were 250,000 to 300,000 homeless people in the United States in 1983 to 1984 (Hagan, 1987) while the National Coalition for the Homeless estimates that there are more than three million homeless people (Rafferty & Rollins, 1989b). The National Alliance to End Homelessness estimated that on any given night in 1988 there were 735,000 homeless people (Levine & Rog, 1990).

The reason for the disparity in the figures may be political, or may be related to methodological differences. Differences in the definition of homelessness affects who is to be counted. Whether the count is an estimate, survey of service providers and shelters, or an actual street count conducted across a period of time or on a given day, affects the outcome. Even the day chosen is a variable according to the weather, time of year, time of month and locale (Hombs & Snyder, 1986; Johnson, 1989). However, regardless of the method used and the number attained, most researchers agree that homelessness is growing and at a very rapid rate between 13 to 50 percent annually (Bassuk, 1984; Hagan, 1987; National Coalition for the Homeless, 1987b, 1989; Johnson & Kreuger, 1989; Ferguson, 1990; Grinspoon, 1990a, 1990b; Rossi, 1990).

Growing Number of Homeless Children and Their Families

Of the more than three million homeless people in the United States, families with children are the fastest growing segment and account for over 40 percent of the homeless population (Ely, 1987; Doolan, Georgedes, Dillman, & Willis, 1989; Edelman & Mihaly, 1989; Hartman, 1989; Mills & Ota, 1989; Rafferty & Rollins, 1989b). The vast majority of these are female-headed families because women and their children are at high risk for homelessness from poverty, and once homeless, have difficulty finding affordable housing (Hagan, 1987). The ranks of homeless people are also being swelled by the 1.8 million women who are physically abused each year. Most of these women bring their children with them when they are placed in shelters for the abused and many later become homeless when they have no place to go or have exhausted their resources (Hagan, 1987; Davidson & Jenkins, 1989).

A Boston study found that the typical homeless family was female-headed with 2.4 children and more than 90 percent were receiving financial aid (Bassuk, 1987). A New York City study had similar findings except families who were not already on public assistance had to apply for public assistance in order to qualify for shelter (Grant, 1990).

The State of New Jersey Department of Education (1989) reported a total of 19,900 homeless youth and children in New Jersey. Based on state projections for 21 counties from a five county sample, they estimated that Monmouth and Middlesex Counties were among the counties most highly populated by homeless people, exceeded by only Bergen and Essex counties. A majority of these homeless youth and children resided in motels or hotels while half as many resided in shelters. In Middlesex County, Catholic Charities (1991) reported that in 1990 at their family shelter in Middlesex County, they provided 24,831 days of care and served 74,493 meals to 655 individuals from 311 families.

As the number of homeless families has increased, so has their average length of stay in temporary homeless facilities (Rafferty & Rollins, 1989a). For these facilities the word temporary may be a misnomer. In 1988, 39 percent of the families had been in New York City shelters for more than one year and ten percent had been in the shelters two years or more (Rafferty & Rollins, 1989a). A study conducted in Ohio found that the families included had been homeless from one to four years (First, Toomey, & Rife, 1990).

Families living in shelters are in a volatile and sometimes violent atmosphere where they feel enormous amounts of stress and have a multitude of problems (Bassuk, 1984; Hutchison, Searight, & Stretch, 1986; Bassuk & Gallagher, 1990; Daly, 1990). Homeless children suffer from malnutrition, developmental delays, depressed language skills, poor self control, behavior problems, nightmares, phobias, food hoarding, psychogenic water drinking, mood disturbances, and other signs of emotional disturbances (Bassuk, 1987; Bassuk & Rubin, 1987; Grant, 1990; Whitman, Accardo, Boyert, & Kendagor, 1990). Often they have been victims or witnesses of some type of abuse or domestic friction before they became homeless (Hutchison, Searight, & Stretch, 1986; Hickson & Gaydon, 1989) and now reside in a shelter where the environment itself can foster more psychological and physical harm (Johnson & Kreuger, 1989).

This kind of life provokes a variety of responses ranging from anger and outrage to guilt, shame and a sense of helplessness (Hartman, 1989) and the child's health, education and emotional development suffer (Edelman & Mihaly, 1989). Yet, with all of these problems, existing research on homelessness and education focuses mostly on children's access to educational services. This literature tends to be descriptive with little empirical data on what happens to children once they are enrolled in school (e.g., Rafferty & Rollins, 1989b).

Problems Experienced by Homeless Children in School

In December 1988, a U.S. Department of Education report (1989) indicated that there were 220,000 homeless children in the United States, of whom 67,000 (30 percent) did not attend school regularly. A New Jersey State Department of Education Report agreed that 30 percent of the state's 19,900 homeless children do not attend school (Doolan, Georgedes, Dillman, & Willis, 1989). According to Advocates for Children these figures grossly underestimate the problem. For example, the National Coalition for the Homeless estimated that at least 57 percent of these children do not attend school regularly (Rafferty & Rollins, 1989a). Molnar (1989) placed the figure at 50 percent while other national studies place the figure at 43 percent (Eddowes & Hranitz, 1989; Ely, 1987; Maza & Hall, 1988; Schumack, 1987). The differences may be due to definition in that another State of New Jersey Department of Education report (1989) stated that more than half of the homeless children do not attend school regularly and another 43 percent attend only irregularly.

To make the problem of school attendance more graphic, erratic attendance can be defined as 4 or more days absent per week. Using that definition, the New York State Department of Education (1988) reported that in 1986, 50 to 55 percent of New York City's homeless elementary school children and 55 percent of New York City's homeless secondary school children met that criteria.

As noted above, the length of time a family might remain homeless has been lengthening and concurrently, the length of stay for a family in a specific homeless facility has also been lengthening. As some studies suggest, shelters are becoming the permanent residence of homeless people (Grinspoon, 1990a; Grunberg & Eagle, 1990). Thus, the transient nature of homelessness may account for very little of the variance in school attendance by homeless children, yet, school attendance continues to be a significant problem. In New York City, 67 percent of all homeless children and 76 percent of homeless high school students have changed schools no more than once since they became homeless (Rafferty & Rollins, 1989a) yet, as noted above, 55 percent of these children had erratic attendance problems. This compares to an average attendance rate for all students of 88.7 percent in elementary school, 85.5 percent in junior high schools and 83.9 percent in high schools in the City of New York.

A 1989 U.S. Department of Education report identified several reasons for the poor school attendance of homeless children. These included lack of health care, the transient nature of homelessness, lack of finances to purchase supplies and clothes for school, lack of access to day care services for school-age parents and the discouragement that accompanies frequent school changes and absences. In addition, the New Jersey plan for state action (1989) and several other state plans (Missouri Department of Elementary & Secondary Education, 1989; New York State Education Department, 1989) identify such educational obstacles as meeting residency requirements, transportation, problems and delays with transferring school and health/immunization records, delays and difficulties in finding appropriate placements and programs, lack of coordination between agencies and service providers, a lack of state monitoring to determine if the needs of the homeless population are being met, a lack of awareness for staff and the public at large, and a lack of supplementary and supportive services (Doolan, Georgedes, Dillman, & Willis, 1989).

Once in school, the school environment is expected to function as a safe haven for homeless children, a place where they can get away from an otherwise stressful environment (Horowitz, Springer, & Kose, 1988; Tower & White, 1989). However, the children become discouraged when they fall behind in their work as a result of frequent school absences and as they get older are at higher risk of dropping out (Grinspoon, 1990a; Rafferty & Rollins, 1989a). Another factor which increases the likelihood of dropping out is repeating a grade; homeless children are more likely to be over-age for their grade (Rafferty & Rollins, 1989b) or to have repeated a grade (Bassuk, 1987). Finally, even experienced teachers may have high less positive attitudes toward their homeless students, the more they have contact with them (Lindley, 1994). School becomes overwhelming and becomes another source of stress in an already stressful world, rather than a haven (Whitman, Accardo, Boyert & Kendagor, 1990). Putting it more simply, school attendance may just also be low on their list of priorities (Stronge & Tenhouse, 1990) and their attitudes toward school have been found to be poor (Winborne & Murray, 1992).

Homeless Children and Their Socialization Difficulties at School

Some studies maintain that it is frequent moves and frequent absences from school that also make it difficult for homeless children to make and keep friends (Eddowes & Hranitz, 1989; Rafferty & Rollins, 1989a; 1989b). Others believe it is a higher level of shyness that makes the homeless child unable to make friends (Roseman & Stein, 1990). Still others believe that homeless children are isolated from their peers during school hours (Horowitz, Springer, & Kose, 1988). Charles Smith, Tennessee Commissioner of Education, believes that homeless children feel rejected by their classmates (Gore, 1990) and being disliked is associated with poor attendance and dropping out of school (Hartup, 1989). In addition, shelter programs do not provide the trappings for social acceptance in school like stylish clothing and modern hair styles (Davidson & Jenkins, 1989). Whatever the factors are that contribute to the difficulties that homeless children have in school, Rafferty and Shinn (1991) in their review of the literature related to those factors concluded that homeless children were at a disadvantage in school and were educational underachievers for a variety of reasons.

Homeless youngsters may have difficulties forming and maintaining friendships, and these friendship difficulties may contribute to further problems especially in school. For example, Grant (1990) speculated that homeless children have experienced so much prior loss in their lives that they entered new relationships in a way that protected them against pain from future loss. Eddowes and Hranitz (1989) related the homeless child's socialization difficulties to Maslow's hierarchy of needs. They felt that homeless children were so concerned with fulfilling their level one and two needs for food, shelter, clothing, safety, and security that they were unable to concern themselves with higher level needs of socialization and acceptance by others. Grunberg and Eagle (1990) believe that homeless people go through a process they call "shelterization" the longer they reside in shelters. This process is characterized by a decrease in interpersonal responsiveness, increasing passivity and increased dependency on others in both adults and children.

Friendships develop when there is an equal power base, common interests, and similarities between self and others. These are horizontal relationships (Hartup, 1989). Sheltered women do not feel equal to shelter staff regardless of how much social status they had before they became homeless (Davidson & Jenkins, 1989). This may also be true and even more so for homeless youngsters since homeless children tend to be older and further behind academically than their classmates, with more emotional problems and stress than their housed peers (e.g., Bassuk, 1987). They also have trouble fitting in because they are also less stylish than their housed peers (e.g., U.S. Department of Education, 1989).

There is also some indication that homeless children are not made welcome in school (Schumack, 1987) by classmates who find it difficult to grasp what it means to have no place that is home (Hartman, 1989). At school they are met by jeers, taunts, and rejection (Eddowes & Hranitz, 1989). A complaint quoted in one of the studies was that "the other kids don't treat the children from the shelter nicely...they pick on them, and call them `the shelter kids' or `the homeless kids'" (Rafferty & Rollins, 1989a: 88). Labels, such as these, influence the child's self-concept and how others react to them (Yuker, 1987). Negative societal attitudes can become a barrier to acceptance (Sales, 1986) causing the socially rejected child to affiliate with other children who share their own antisocial attitudes and further isolate themselves (Hartup, 1989). These negative attitudes that the children in school have toward a homeless child, may be caused in part by the stereotypes and prejudices the children may have been exposed to at home, in the media, or by friends.

Stereotypes About Homeless Children

A stereotype is a generalization about a group of people that distinguishes those people from others (Myers, 1990). When homelessness was studied from a semantic and sociological point of view, it was found that the various terms used in the media in different countries to describe the homeless population, were mostly stigmatizing (Gagne & Dorvil, 1988). The press, television, and the movies have an enormous impact on knowledge, attitudes and public policies regarding a variety of issues and may be filled with stereotypical and inappropriate portrayals. These negative portrayals may influence our perceptions and our actions towards others for a long time (Keller, Hallahan, McShane, Crowley, & Blanford, 1990).

Approximately ten years ago it was felt the media portrayed homeless people as "expendable" people who were nothing more than parasites who choose to live in the streets a la "Billy Boggs" (Hopper, 1984). At that time many politicians felt the government had little obligation to care for homeless people (Bassuk, 1984) and portrayed the needy as undeserving. Then, through a process of devaluation, they became easier to scapegoat (Staub, 1996). Some individuals may have felt more charitable but their attitude changed after they have repeatedly been aggressively panhandled (Ferguson, 1990).

In 1989 and 1990 an extensive survey on homelessness was conducted in a northeast city by Toro and McDonell (1992). They found that there was neither a distinct negative nor positive attitude towards homeless people among their adult respondents but, admitted that other studies were beginning to suggest that Americans were becoming less supportive toward the poor and that the media was in the process of shifting public opinion against homeless people. Other researchers feel that a class confrontation is brewing between angry homeless people and citizens who are supporting legislation across the country to take back the streets and parks from homeless people (Ferguson, 1990).

Society in general views homeless children and youths as either victims who need to be rescued, delinquents who need to be disciplined, or as individuals whose existence is to be ignored (Stronge & Tenhouse, 1990). Miel (cited in Byrnes, 1988) found that class bias by socioeconomic status (SES), discrimination against the unattractive, and biases against certain lifestyles, all involve prejudicial and discriminatory behaviors that have been found in elementary school children. This is because association with out-group (homeless) individuals may be detrimental to one's standing within the in-group and children are very susceptible to biases from significant others in their world. In-groups, by their very nature, lay the groundwork for prejudice and discrimination by admitting and excluding others, and their attitudes become the reference points by which the out-group is judged (Sherman, 1990).

In fact, stereotyping and labeling by teachers and peers was found to be a common phenomenon with children becoming more isolated as a result of the cycle of labeling, reactivity, and more labeling (Whitman, Accardo, Boyert, & Kendagor, 1990). Homeless children who do make it to school are often stigmatized by their peers and sometimes by their teachers because of their different appearance, dress, social norms, and poor academic performance (Stronge & Tenhouse, 1990). Educators have lower expectations for disadvantaged children such as homeless children, creating a self-fulfilling prophecy where standards are set at a level not high enough to form a foundation for future academic success (Knapp & Shields, 1990). The more contact teachers have with homeless students, the less positive their attitudes (Lindley, 1994).

Prejudice Toward Homeless Children

Prejudice is an unjustifiable negative attitude toward a group (such as homeless children) and its individual members, and is characterized by preconceived opinions or feelings that are without merit (Myers, 1990). Even though prejudice is no longer fashionable, there are several indications that racial prejudice still exists underground, surfacing when it is safe, not when a behavior would look prejudicial but when it can hide behind some other motive (Pine & Hilliard, 1990). Prejudices fulfill the psychological and social needs of the individuals who hold them and are often perpetuated and supported by the community (Byrnes, 1988). For instance, poor people feel less threatened by street youths than do wealthier families (Apetekar, 1990) but, age and level of education are also factors (Benjamin, 1989).

Allport (cited in Damico, Bell-Nathaniel, & Green, 1981; Sherman, 1990) and later Cohen (cited in Damico, Bell-Nathaniel, & Green, 1981) used contact theory and applied it to schools to explain prejudice. They believe that if schools are structured to promote equal status and interdependent and cooperative contact between students of different races, then students will have more opposite race friends than will students in traditionally organized schools. Claney and Parker (1989) agreed. They found that Whites who were well acquainted with Blacks were more comfortable with Blacks than Whites who had had less contact. Unfortunately, they also found that Whites who held extreme attitudes towards Blacks were also more comfortable in their dealings with Blacks. Carter (1990) on the other hand, found that White men at all levels of racial awareness held racist beliefs while White women had racist beliefs when their awareness was low. Others found that White undergraduates associated positive traits more with Whites than with Blacks and negative characteristics more with Blacks than with Whites (Dovidio, Evans, & Taylor, 1986).

These studies suggest that the attitudes of housed school children towards their homeless peers are important because they may effect how homeless children feel about coming to school. As noted above, homeless children are not welcomed by their housed peers in school (Schumack, 1987) and are often teased by them (Eddowes & Hranitz, 1989; Rafferty & Rollins, 1989a; Stronge & Tenhouse, 1990).

Poverty And Attitudes Toward Homeless Children

The Congress of the United States, Committee on Ways and Means (1985) reported that children are now the poorest age group in the United States. In 1987, 20.6 percent of American children, 13 million, were poor (Plotnick, 1989) and therefore at risk for homelessness. In 1989 it was estimated that one child in four was growing up in poverty and it was noted that the United States is the first nation in history where children are the poorest segment of the population (Molnar, 1989). Elementary school children have been found to be biased against and to discriminate against classmates who were from lower social strata or had poorer lifestyles (Miel, cited in Byrnes, 1988).

Is it "homelessness" or is it "poverty" that causes the socialization problems homeless children face when they come to school and can the two be separated? Almost all homeless people are impoverished and therefore one would expect there to be many similarities between poor and homeless children. The House Select Committee on Children, Youth, and Families (Congress of the United States, 1989) found that poverty affects families with higher suicide rates, increased violence, hunger, homelessness and familial separation in order to find work. Poverty is correlated with a number of factors such as premature birth, poor health and nutrition, compromised development, failure to develop trusting relationships early in life, child abuse, and school related stress (Chafel, 1990).

When matched samples of homeless and housed poor families were compared it was found that in both groups, many of the mothers had little work experience and had been on welfare for long periods. Most of the children in both groups had serious developmental and emotional problems (Bassuk & Rosenberg, 1988). No significant differences were found between the mean achievement scores of homeless children and a matched sample of poor housed peers (Marcus, Flatter, Talabis, Ford, Conahan, & Catoe, 1991), nor were mean differences found in terms of how far they expected to go in school, or the status of occupations they aspired to (Martagon, Ramirez, & Masten, 1991). Rescola, Parker, and Stolley (1991) concluded that when viewed as groups, homeless children and their poor housed peers did not differ significantly on most measures. Poverty was found to be a key mediator of developmental problems for both homeless and poor children when compared to normative samples and studies have found that poverty and homelessness specifically, was related to the development of psychological problems (Rafferty & Shinn, 1991).

It is not surprising that as noted above, poor children whether housed or homeless are similar because both groups have experienced the effects of poverty. Recent studies have emphasized these similarities because both groups are at high risk to develop problems, but homeless children clearly do worse than their housed peers (Rafferty & Shinn, 1991). The differences that are found between the two groups of children may be attributable to the homelessness that only one group has experienced.

Alperstein, Rappaport, and Flanigan (1988) compared housed and homeless poor children and found that homeless children had elevated blood levels, more hospital admissions, and were victims of abuse and neglect more frequently. Other studies have found that homeless children show more behavior problems and more aggressive and acting-out behaviors than their poor housed peers (Rescola, Parker, & Stolley, 1991). Their parents have been arrested and have attempted suicide more frequently and are more likely to have been hospitalized for alcohol or psychiatric problems (Bassuk & Rosenberg, 1988; Linn, Gelberg, & Leake, 1990). These children are also higher than poor housed children in shyness, dependent behaviors, attention deficiencies, withdrawal, and demanding behaviors (Roseman & Stein, 1990).

When evaluated, homeless children have been found to function intellectually in the borderline range at a three times higher rate than the poor housed population and to have significant language delays (Whitman, Accardo, Boyert, & Kendagor, 1990). They had serious developmental and emotional problems to the extent that more than half required psychiatric evaluations (Bassuk & Rosenberg, 1988; Bassuk & Rubin, 1987; Bassuk, Rubin, & Lauriet, 1986; Grant, 1990). Homeless adults and children have also been found to have lower self esteem and significantly higher levels of depression than the poor housed population (Bassuk & Rubin, 1987; Belcher & DiBlasio, 1990).

These studies raise an important issue about how poor homeless children might be viewed by their peers in school. Some studies show that poverty has a similar effect on children whether housed or homeless (Bassuk & Rosenberg, 1988; Marcus, Flatter, Talabis, Ford, Conahan, & Catoe, 1991; Martagon, Ramirez, & Masten, 1991; Rescorla, Parker, & Stolley, 1991), while others have shown significant differences (Alperstein, Rappaport, & Flanigan, 1988; Bassuk & Rosenberg, 1988; Linn, Gelberg, & Leake, 1990), particularly in areas that might influence acceptance by peers in school (e.g., Bassuk & Rubin, 1987; Roseman & Stein, 1990; Rescola, Parker, & Stolley, 1991).

Ethnicity And Attitudes Toward Homeless Children

Homeless people are a stigmatized group not only because of their poverty but also because of the stereotype that they are non-White (Somerman, 1990). In studies where ethnicity was reported, it was generally found that minorities were overrepresented in the population of homeless families and were at greater risk to become homeless (Hombs & Snyder, 1986; First, Roth, & Arewa, 1988; Johnson & Kreuger, 1989; National Coalition for the Homeless, 1989; Grant, 1990). Minorities, particularly Blacks, comprise more than 50 percent of the homeless population nationally (First, Roth, & Arewa, 1988; National Coalition for the Homeless, 1989). The image of the homeless population has changed from that of an old skid row bum with his hand extended for change to young Black and Hispanic men angry at the lack of good paying jobs who demand money from passersby (Ferguson, 1990).

These prejudices are carried into school according to Hilliard (as cited in Pine & Hilliard, 1990). He feels that educational outcomes and the educational process are different for the various racial, economic, and gender groups in the United States. Arciniega (as cited in Pine & Hilliard, 1990) believes that this is because schools are designed to serve the English speaking, White, middle class student. When asked, Black students revealed that they too believe that schools are geared toward the White middle class (Polakow-Suransky & Ulaby, 1990; Thompson, et al., 1990). Thomas and Lee (1990) found that this was true not only for ethnic minorities but also for disabled people, although at times disabled people were viewed more sympathetically. The performance judgments of elementary school teachers were affected by the race and social class of the students and racial bias persisted even after intelligence information was given. The teachers went so far as to report that they felt that their biases were reliable predictors of future success (McCombs & Gay, 1988).

Glock (as cited in Sherman, 1990) found that racial and social class prejudice is widespread in our schools, particularly our high schools and colleges where a resurgence of racial harassment and violence against Black students has been reported (Farrell & Jones, 1988; Polakow-Suransky & Ulaby, 1990). When high school students were surveyed, White students resented the feelings of anger and bitterness they felt Black students were expressing toward them and had a perception that minorities had privileged opportunities for scholarships and college admission (Polakow-Suransky & Ulaby, 1990).

Peer groups are often formed along racial and class lines. Students in integrated classes in middle schools typically resegregate themselves when they socialize in the lunchroom and is believed by some to be an indicator of prejudice (Sager & Schofield, 1980; Schofield, 1982, 1986). Racial prejudice is a function of one's family where a child is predisposed to the parent's values and prejudices (Sherman, 1990). Tracking also separates students not only by academic ability but also by SES and race (Polakow-Suransky & Ulaby, 1990). Race and SES may have an impact upon the attitudes that middle class children have towards their homeless peers. As was noted above, peer groups in schools tend to form along SES and racial lines (Sager & Schofield, 1980; Schofield, 1982, 1986), tracking separates students not only by academic ability but also by SES and race (Polakow-Suransky & Ulaby, 1990), and significant incidents of social and/or racial prejudice have been reported (Farrell & Jones, 1988; Polakow-Suransky & Ulaby, 1990).

It has already been shown that from 30 to more than 50 percent of homeless children do not attend school regularly (Rafferty & Rollins, 1989a; U.S. Department of Education, 1989), do poorly when they attend (Bassuk, 1987; Rafferty & Rollins, 1989b; Grinspoon, 1990a), and feel rejected by their classmates when they do attend school (Gore, 1990). This study will investigate whether children in school have negative attitudes toward their homeless peers and whether those attitudes are affected by poverty or racial prejudices.

Based upon the literature reviewed, the following hypotheses are formulated:

Research Hypotheses

1. Nonpoor housed children in grades six through twelve, will have significantly more positive attitudes toward a nonpoor, housed peer than toward a poor, housed peer.

2. Nonpoor housed children in grades six through twelve, will have significantly more positive attitudes toward a nonpoor, housed peer than a poor, homeless peer.

3. Nonpoor housed children in grades six through twelve, will have significantly more positive attitudes toward a poor, housed peer than toward a poor, homeless peer.

Although many studies have found a number of similarities between poor housed and poor homeless people (Congress of the United States, 1989; Chafel, 1990; Marcus, Flatter, Talabis, Ford, Conahan, & Catoe, 1991; Rescorla, Parker, & Stolley, 1991), many studies have found a number of differences between the two groups (Bassuk & Rosenberg, 1988; Linn, Gelberg, & Leake, 1990; Whitman, Accardo, Boyert, & Kendagor, 1990). Many of these differences were in areas which might directly affect how easily they made and kept friends (Bassuk & Rubin, 1987; Belcher & DiBlasio, 1990; Roseman & Stein, 1990) or in behavioral areas which might affect how others viewed them (Rescorla, Parker, & Stolley, 1991).

4. Nonpoor, housed, school-age children will prefer to associate more closely with a nonpoor, housed peer than with a poor, housed peer.

5. Nonpoor, housed, school-age children will prefer to associate more closely with a nonpoor, housed peer than a poor, homeless peer.

6. Nonpoor, housed, school-age children will prefer to associate more closely with a poor, housed peer than with a poor, homeless peer.

Research that supports these hypotheses was conducted by Miel (cited in Byrnes, 1988) who found that elementary school children were biased against and discriminated against classmates who were from lower social strata or had poorer lifestyles. When out-group status was based on poverty, association with out-group peers was detrimental to one's standing in the in-group and therefore very susceptible to the biases of the in-group (Sherman, 1990). Other research has shown that homeless children have more difficulty making and keeping friends and are rejected by their classmates. They are not welcomed by their classmates and are often met with ridicule (Eddowes & Hranitz, 1989; Rafferty & Rollins, 1989a, 1989b; Gore,1990).

Research Questions

In addition to the above hypotheses, the following research questions will be addressed. 1) Will ethnicity interact with attitudes toward poverty and homelessness? 2) Will nonpoor, housed, school-age children have more positive attitudes and prefer to associate more closely with same race (White) students than other race students (Black) across all levels of poverty and housing status?

These questions are supported by the research of Hilliard (as cited in Pine & Hilliard III, 1990) who found that racial differences had a significant affect on the processes that occur in the educational setting. McCombs and Gay (1988) found that both racial and social class factors affected how students were viewed in school while other studies have noted that peer groups are formed along racial and social class lines (Sager & Schofield, 1980; Schofield, 1982, 1986).

II
Method

Subjects

The sample for this study was comprised of 158 White students (see Table 1). They ranged from grades six through twelve with a mean grade of 8.6 (SD = 2.06) and ranged in age from 12 through 18 years with a mean age of 14.3 years (SD = 1.98). There were 85 males (53.8%) and 73 (46.2%) females of whom 92% resided in a residence owned and 8% resided in a residence rented by their parents or their legal guardians. None of the subjects had ever been homeless themselves but six subjects (3.8%) had a family member who had experienced homelessness and 22 subjects (13.3%) reported they knew someone who was or had been homeless (these numbers include the six with family members). Subjects were chosen from the Middle School, Junior High School, and High School from a community in Middlesex County, New Jersey. Two social studies classes from each grade, six through twelve, were randomly selected from the four to six social studies classes on each grade. The school system services approximately 6800 students (3800 in grades six through twelve) of which approximately 80 percent are White, 14.5 percent are Asian, 2.5 percent are Black, 2.5 percent are Hispanic and 0.5 percent are "other".

The community selected is an ethnically mixed, middle class suburban community located approximately 15 to 20 miles southwest of New York City. The community is comprised mostly of professionals and semi-professionals where approximately 75% of the students enroll in post-secondary programs. Of the approximately 6,800 students enrolled in the school district, no more than 5 percent of the children currently enrolled are homeless.

Materials and Instruments

For this study, nonpoor housed people were referred to as "middle class" in the experimental measures and defined as those who own or pay rent for the facility in which they live. Poor housed people were defined as those who own or rent the facility in which they live but who have incomes low enough to qualify for free lunch in school. Homeless people were defined as

Table 1

Sociodemographic Characteristics of the Sample (n=158)

	Number	Mean	SD	Percentage
Age		14.29	1.98	
Grade		8.59	2.06	
six	40			25.3%
seven	18			11.4%
eight	14			8.9%
nine	27			17.1%
ten	21			13.3%
eleven	23			14.6%
twelve	15			9.5%
Male	85			53.8%
Female	73			46.2%
Ever Homeless Themselves	0			0.0
Any Family Member Ever Homeless	6			3.80%
Know Anyone Who Was Ever Homeless	20			12.66%
Own the Home In Which They Live	145			91.77%
Rent the Home In Which They Live	13			8.23%

those who have no permanent place of residence or reside in facilities provided by the state welfare department.

Attitudes toward homeless peers, poor peers and nonpoor housed peers were measured by a revised version of the Attitude and Belief Scale (ABS) as developed by Marks (1992). This is a scale that was originally designed to measure the attitudes of health care workers toward homeless people. It was adapted here for six treatment conditions (middle class, poor, and homeless by Black and White) to reflect the school setting (Appendix A). All questions were essentially kept the same in terms of intent although some rewording was required because of the age and possible reading levels of the youngest subjects. As an example, question five on the original version referred to "reinstitutionalization". Based upon interviews with several respondents in a pilot study, this was reworded to read, "put them into institutions" to increase readability and understanding. (The pilot study is described in more detail on pages 31-32.) The ABS consisted of 28 items with six Likert scale choices for each item scored one to six points each. The possible range of scores was from 28 to 168 points, where higher scores indicated more negative attitudes. Cronbach's alpha for Marks' version was .90 (1992) while for this version of the ABS and this sample it was .87 indicating adequate overall internal consistency. The Spearman-Brown split-half odd-even reliability for the version used here was .54.

The decision to use the ABS was made as the result of a pilot study that compared the Social Skills Rating System (SSRS; Gresham & Elliot, 1990), the California F Scales (Adorno, Levinson, Frenkel-Brunswik, & Sanford, 1950), and the Attitude and Belief Scales. The study was conducted to identify the best measure of attitudes towards homeless people. The pilot included ten students, ranging from grades six through twelve, who resided in the community in which the entire study was conducted.

Twice as many of the pilot study subjects (six) rated the ABS easier to use and as the best measure of attitudes. The SSRS was the next most preferred measure. In comparing the measures, little difference was found as to ease of understanding the directions. Although the respondents, when asked directly, professed to understand the questions approximately equally well on all three measures, questions were not responded to on 50% of the F scale protocols, 40% of the SSRS protocols and 30% of the ABS protocols. The mean number of questions left blank was 4.3 out of 39 (11%) on the SSRS and 4.3 out of 30 (14%) on the F scales. Of the 30 questions on the ABS, a mean of 1.1 (3.6%) questions were not responded to. This occurred most frequently on question five which was reworded as noted above.

The large percentage of respondents who failed to answer all of the questions and the large percentage of questions skipped, made it impossible to score the protocols. This contributed to the elimination of the F scale and SSRS as possible measures to be included in this study.

A semantic differential scale (SemD) that also measured attitudes toward nonpoor housed, poor housed, and homeless peers was administered, as a validity check to ensure that the subjects were interpreting the material presented, as predicted, as well as for future study. This SemD (see Appendix C) uses a seven point rating scale because it has been shown that with seven choices, the choices tend to be used with generally more equal frequency. It is comprised of 20 pairs of adjectives. Half the items begin with the complimentary adjective and half the items begin with the derogatory adjective. (Kidder, Judd, & Smith, 1986; Osgood, Suci, & Tannenbaum, 1957). The 20 items were scored from one to seven with a score of one being assigned to the most positive position and seven to the most negative. The scores therefore ranged from 20 to 140 with higher scores indicating a more negative attitude toward the group being rated.

Willingness to associate with homeless peers was measured by a Social Distance Scale (SocD). Social distance is a measure of the degree of understanding and feeling that people have toward each other. It is used to explain the nature of their interactions and the character of their social relations (Bogardus, 1925, 1933, 1939). It has been used successfully in studies involving children ages 12 to 17 (Bogardus, 1937). Campbell (as cited in Buros, 1970) found that the SDS is one of the most popular tests of social attitudes and that it has been used by many well known researchers subsequent to Bogardus's research. He reported that split-half reliabilities range from .94 to .97. The version of the SocD used in this study was developed specifically for use by students to assess their racial attitudes (Zeligs & Hendrickson, 1933, 1935; Zeligs, 1936).

In this version of the SocD (Appendix B), the respondent is required to write either yes or no in each of the spaces following the name of each group according to whether they would be willing or unwilling to have a member of the group as a best friend, friend, playmate, classmate, or schoolmate. It was scored by the percentage of "yes" responses of total responses and as a Guttman scale (Bellows, 1961) yielding scores that could possibly range from zero percent to 100 percent with lower scores indicating less willingness to associate with a given group. Blocks that are left blank by respondents, were not scored and were not included in computing percentages. In the current version, the five categories of association/social distance were selected because these categories are more meaningful for American students and the differences between them were approximately equally distant.

Two social studies classes from each grade (six through twelve) were randomly selected for the study. The number of social studies classes varied from grade to grade. There were four classes in grade six, five classes in grades seven and eight, and six classes in grades nine through twelve. Within each class the subjects were randomly assigned to one of six conditions. In each condition they received a packet comprised of a sociodemographic data sheet and one of the six versions of the ABS which they responded to first, the same version of the SemD which they responded to next, and the SocD which they responded to last. In each condition the subject was asked to rate, on each of the measures provided, people described as being either nonpoor housed, poor housed, or homeless and for each of these conditions, the people were described as being either ethnically White or Black.

Design

This experiment had two independent variables, type of peer with three levels: nonpoor housed, poor housed, or homeless; and ethnicity of peer with two levels: Black or White. It was a between subjects design.

The independent variables were:

I. Type of peer:

Level 1 - Nonpoor Housed
Level 2 - Poor Housed
Level 3 - Homeless

II. Ethnicity of peer:

Level 1 - Black
Level 2 - White

Procedure

The school district in which the study was run requested that after the subjects were selected they (if they were over 18 years of age), or their parents, would be asked to sign an informed consent form (Appendix D) prior to the experiment. Following the experiment they were offered to have a copy of the results distributed to them when the study was completed. Following *all* data collection the subjects were debriefed.

The subjects were randomly assigned to one of the two levels (Black or White) of the three conditions (Nonpoor Housed, Poor Housed, or Homeless). Each subject was given a sealed, unmarked manila envelope containing the three measures described above. The measures were numbered with the ABS first, the SemD second, and the SocD third. They were instructed as follows:

> You are going to participate in an experiment to see how
> students feel about other types of students they might encounter in
> school. Please fill out the measures in the order in which they are

presented in your packet. Read the directions carefully and answer all the questions. If you find it difficult to answer some of the questions, please answer the questions anyway based on what you know or believe about the group described. Once you have finished a measure you cannot go back and change your answers. Let me know when you are finished. Thank you.

The only identifying information that was collected was the subject's gender, date of birth, school, grade, ethnicity, whether their parent(s)/guardian(s) rented or owned their residence, and whether they have ever experienced homelessness first hand, in the immediate family, or whether they knew or had met someone who was homeless. The experimenter distributing the sealed packet to each subject was blind as to which condition each subject was receiving.

After the measures were completed, they were collected by the experimenter. At a follow-up session after *all* data had been collected, the purpose of the study was explained to the subjects, they were debriefed and questions answered.

Statistical Analysis

Split-half reliability and Cronbach's alpha were calculated for the scores obtained on the ABS. This was to determine if this version of the ABS had sufficient internal consistency.

A correlation analysis (see Appendix E) was computed to determine if there are any unpredicted relationships between independent variables. Pearson's product moment correlations were used for all interval scale data (Appendix E) which included all results except for the Guttman Scale data on the SocD. In that the Guttman scale yields rank order data, Spearman correlations were used for its correlational analysis (see Appendix F).

A correlational analysis was performed for the scores obtained on both the ABS and the SocD. Further correlational analysis was done for both of these measures and the subject's age because there is some evidence in the literature that stereotypes and prejudices become stronger with age and are effected by gender (Benjamin, 1989; Toro & McDonell, 1992). The scores obtained on these measures were also subjected to correlational analysis with grade, whether they had ever been homeless, had ever had a homeless family member, or knew anyone who had ever been homeless, and home ownership/home rental to determine if any of these factors were responsible for spurious effects. No significant correlations were found (see Appendix E).

The mean scores obtained on both the ABS and the SocD were separately subjected to 3 (Type of peer with three levels: nonpoor housed, poor housed, and homeless) X 2 (Ethnicity of peer with two levels: Black and

White) ANOVAs to determine if any of the relationships were significant. The following planned comparisons were tested for significance:

Nonpoor Housed	vs.	Poor Housed
Nonpoor Housed	vs.	Homeless
Poor Housed	vs.	Homeless
White Nonpoor Housed	vs.	Black Nonpoor Housed
White Poor Housed	vs.	Black Poor Housed
White Homeless	vs.	Black Homeless

Due to the number of planned comparisons the alpha level ($p = .01$) was adjusted ($p = .008$) to control for the possibility of a Type I error. When the hypotheses are nonorthogonal the modified Bonferroni test is recommended for this purpose (Keppel, 1982).

A correlational analysis was conducted for scores obtained on the SemD with scores obtained on the ABS and the SocD (see Appendixes E and F). It was found that the relationships were positive and significant for the ABS and negative and significant for the SocD. The higher the score on the ABS and the SemD, the more negative the attitude, while the higher the score on the SocD, the more the subject was willing to associate.

III

Results

Introduction

This results chapter is divided into three sections. The first subsection discusses the hypotheses on attitudes toward different types of peers and the results obtained from both the Attitude and Belief Scale and the Semantic Differential Scale. The second subsection addresses the hypotheses on willingness to associate with different types of peers and the results obtained from the SocD. The last subsection reviews the results that relate to the research questions. These questions proposed that ethnicity would be a factor in the attitudes of White adolescent children toward different types of peers and preferences pertaining to the types of peers with whom they would associate.

The Attitude and Belief Scale (see Appendix A) was administered to measure the attitudes of the children toward their peers. The Semantic Differential Scale (see Appendix C) was originally administered only as a validity check to help determine if the Attitude and Belief Scale was measuring what it was proported to measure. After it was determined that this correlation was significant (see Appendix E), it was decided to also subject the data from the Semantic Differential Scale to the same statistical analysis as the Attitude and Belief Scale to determine if it would yield the same results.

Attitudes Toward Peers

Attitudes toward nonpoor housed (NPH), poor housed (PH), and homeless (HL) children were measured using the ABS. An analysis of variance (3 X 2 ANOVA) was performed on the mean scores obtained from this measure. As can be seen in Table 2, the simple main effects test was significant for housing status ($F_{2,152} = 5.92, p = .003$). Further analysis of the data indicates that nonpoor housed children in grades six through twelve have significantly more positive attitudes toward a NPH peer than toward a PH peer as was hypothesized in the first hypothesis (see Table 4). The subjects' mean score on the ABS was 65.72 ($SD = 15.85$) for a NPH peer as compared to 68.88 ($SD = 15.12$) for a PH peer (see Table 5). Further, nonpoor housed children have

Table 2

Simple Main Effects Test for Attitudes toward Different Types of Peers (Attitude and Belief Scale Scores) (n=158)

Source of Variation	SS	DF	MS	F	p
Ethnicity	2072.374	1	2072.374	6.630	.011
Housing Status	3702.886	2	1851.443	5.923	.003
Ethnicity X Housing	73.207	2	86.604	.277	.758
Error	47512.670	152	312.583		
Total	53595.222	157	341.371		

Table 3

Simple Main Effects Test for Attitudes toward Different Types of Peers (Semantic Differential Scale Scores) (n=158)

Source of Variation	SS	DF	MS	F	p
Ethnicity	571.511	1	571.511	1.921	.168
Housing Status	12444.649	2	6222.325	20.916	<.001
Ethnicity X Housing	1424.796	5	2903.421	9.760	<.001
Error	45218.697	152	297.491		
Total	59735.804	157	380.483		

Table 4

Mean Comparison Tests of Significance for Attitudes toward
Different Types of Peers (ABS Data) (n=158)

Comparison			t	df	p[a]
HL	vs.	NPH + PH	-3.12	156	.002
PH	vs.	NPH	-2.42	103	.02

Note. [a] Two tailed.
HL = homeless peers
NPH = nonpoor housed peers
PH = poor housed

Table 5

Attitude and Belief (ABS) Scale Mean Scores and Standard Deviations (n=158)

		TYPE OF PEER			
		Nonpoor Housed	Poor Housed	Homeless	Total
ETHNICITY OF PEER	Black	69.96 (19.55)	73.12 (13.71)	79.31 (24.01)	74.22 (19.73)
	White	60.96 (10.23)	64.65 (16.41)	75.00 (16.82)	66.73 (14.79)
	Total	65.72 (15.85)	68.88 (15.12)	77.36 (21.06)	70.66 (18.48)

Note: Numbers in parentheses are standard deviations.
Higher scores indicate a more negative attitude.

significantly more positive attitudes toward a NPH peer than a HL peer as was hypothesized in the second hypothesis (see Table 4). Table 5 shows a mean ABS score of 65.72 (*SD* = 15.85) for a NPH peer as compared to 77.36 (*SD* = 21.06) for a HL peer. The third hypothesis indicated that nonpoor housed children would have significantly more positive attitudes toward a PH peer than toward a HL peer and this difference in mean scores, as obtained on the ABS, was also found to be significant (see Tables 4 and 5).

The SemD which also measured subjects' attitudes toward NPH, PH, and HL children, was originally administered as a validity check for the ABS. The mean scores on this measure.were also subjected to an analysis of variance and results similar to those for the ABS were obtained (see Table 3). The simple main effects test was also significant for housing status ($F_{2,152}$= 20.92, *p* < .001). These results support hypotheses one, two, and three as well. Nonpoor housed children have significantly more positive attitudes toward a NPH peer than toward a PH peer as was hypothesized in the first hypothesis. The mean SemD score was 69.57 (*SD* = 17.38) for a NPH peer as compared to 81.23 (*SD* = 15.53) for a PH peer (see Table 6). Further, nonpoor housed children had significantly more positive attitudes toward a NPH peer than a HL peer ($\underline{F}_{2,152}$ = 20.92, p < .001) as was hypothesized in the second hypothesis (see Table 3). Table 6 shows a mean SemD score of 69.57 (*SD* = 17.38) for a NPH peer as compared to 91.28 (*SD* = 17.61) for a HL peer. The third hypothesis indicated that nonpoor housed children would have significantly more positive attitudes toward a PH peer than toward a HL peer and this difference in mean scores, as obtained on the SemD, was also found to be significant ($F_{2,152}$ = 20.92, *p* < .001) (see Tables 3 and 6).

Willingness to Associate With Nonpoor Housed, Poor Housed, and Homeless Peers

The SocD was used to evaluate the degree to which nonpoor housed children would be willing to associate with Black (B) and White (W) peers of different housing status. The measure was scored as an interval scale and as a Guttman scale. The results were the same for both methods of scoring (see Tables 7 and 8 and Appendixes G and H); therefore only the interval data will be discussed here.

It was found that nonpoor housed children preferred to associate significantly more closely with a NPH peer (*M* = 88.77, *SD* = 22.67) than with a PH peer (*M* = 79.21, *SD* = 27.91) as was stated in hypothesis four or a HL peer (*M* = 63.36, *SD* = 22.67) as was stated in hypothesis five. The sixth hypothesis indicated that nonpoor housed children would prefer to associate significantly more closely with a PH peer (*M* = 79.21, *SD* = 27.91) than a HL

Table 6

Semantic Differential Scale (SemD) Mean Scores and Standard Deviations (n=158)

| | | TYPE OF PEER | | | |
		Nonpoor Housed	Poor Housed	Homeless	Total
ETHNICITY OF PEER	Black	74.36 (19.26)	79.08 (17.29)	93.76 (20.22)	82.61 (19.02)
	White	64.20 (14.99)	83.38 (13.55)	88.29 (13.97)	78.56 (14.18)
	Total	69.57 (17.38)	81.23 (15.53)	91.28 (17.61)	80.69 (16.93)

Note. Numbers in parentheses are standard deviations.
Higher scores indicate a more negative attitude. Table 7

Table 7

Mean Comparison Tests of Significance for Willingness to Associate with Different Types of Peers (SocD Interval Data) (n=158)

Comparison			t	df	p^a
NPH	vs.	PH	6.73	157	<.001
NPH	vs.	HL	11.95	157	<.001
PH	vs.	HL	9.59	157	<.001
WNPH	vs.	BNPH	4.68	157	<.001
WPH	vs.	BPH	4.24	157	<.001
WHL	vs.	BHL	3.61	157	<.001

Note. Modified Bonferroni adjusted alpha for .01, p<.008.
[a] Two tailed.

Table 8

Social Distance Scale Interval Data Mean Scores and Standard Deviations (n=158)

| | | TYPE OF PEER | | | |
		Nonpoor Housed	Poor Housed	Homeless	Total
ETHNICITY OF PEER	Black	85.00 (25.61)	76.01 (29.17)	60.57 (32.99)	73.86 (29.26)
	White	92.53 (19.74)	82.41 (26.65)	66.14 (32.26)	80.36 (26.21)
	Total	88.77 (22.67)	79.21 (27.91)	63.36 (32.62)	77.11 (27.73)

Note. Numbers in parentheses are standard deviations.
Higher scores indicate more positive attitudes.

peer (M = 63.36, SD = 22.67). Table 7 indicates that all three of these comparisons were found to be significant (modified Bonferroni adjusted alpha for .01, $p < .008$). The SocD mean scores and standard deviations are reported in Table 8.

Ethnicity of Peer as a Factor

The first research question queried whether ethnicity would interact with attitudes toward poverty and homelessness. Although the interaction between ethnicity and housing status was not significant on the ABS (see Table 2 and Figure 1) the interaction was significant ($F_{5,152}$ = 9.76, $p < .001$) for the SemD (see Table 3). Mean scores and standard deviations for this measure are reported in Table 6 and graphed in Figure 2. This figure shows that nonpoor, housed children felt significantly more positive towards WNPH (M = 64.20, SD = 14.99) than they did toward BNPH peers (M = 74.36, SD = 19.26). When WHL peers (M = 88.29, SD = 13.97) were compared to BHL peers (M = 93.76, SD = 20.22) and BPH peers (M = 79.08, SD = 17.29) were compared to WPH peers (M = 83.38, SD = 13.55) the differences between the means was not found to be significant.

The second research question inquired as to whether White, nonpoor, housed, children would have more positive attitudes and prefer to associate more closely with same race peers (White) or other race peers (Black) across all levels of poverty and housing status. Attitudinal data (means and standard deviations) for ethnicity as measured by the ABS is reported in Table 5 and was significant ($F_{1,152}$ = 6.630, $p = .011$) as shown in Tables 2 and 9. These data indicate that the subjects had more positive attitudes toward WNPH peers (M = 60.96, SD = 10.23) than BNPH peers (M = 69.96, SD = 19.55) and toward WPH peers (M = 64.65, SD = 16.41) than BPH peers. This relationship can be seen graphically in Figure 1. When attitudes towards HL peers were compared by race, the mean difference between B and W peers was not significant.

When attitudes were measured by the SemD the results were similar but differed in one respect. On this measure, the analysis of variance was not significant for ethnicity ($F_{1,152}$ = 1.921, $p = .168$) but, the subjects did have significantly more positive attitudes toward WNPH peers (M = 64.20, SD =14.99) than BNPH peers (M = 74.36, SD = 19.26) (see Tables 6 and 10). When PH and HL peers mean scores were compared by race, the mean differences were not found to be significant (see Tables 6 and 9).

Willingness to associate was measured by the SocD. For each level of housing status the mean score on the SocD was higher for W peers than for B peers (see Table 8). When the means were tested for significance, it was found that the differences between all three pairs of mean differences were significant

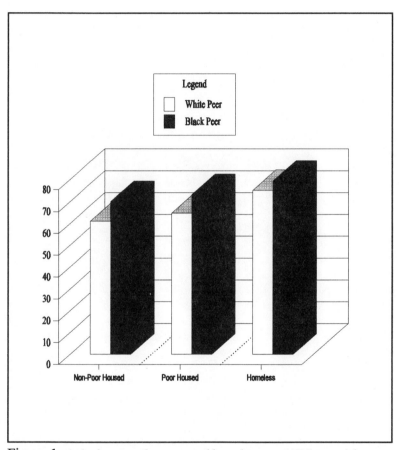

Figure 1. Attitudes toward poverty and homelessness (ABS scores) by
ethnicity of peer (n=158)

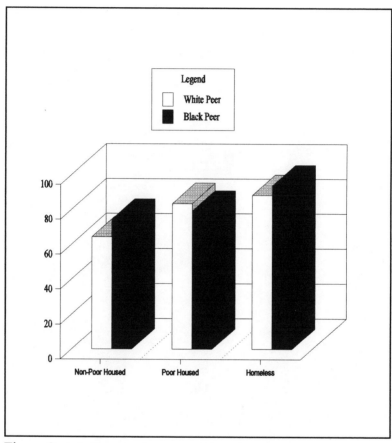

Figure 2. Attitudes toward poverty and homelessness (SemD scores) by ethnicity of peer (n=158)

Table 9

Mean Comparison Tests of Significance for Attitudes toward
Different Types of Peers (ABS Data) (n=158)

Comparison			t	df	p^a
BNPH	vs.	WNPH	2.09	51	.04
BPH	vs.	WPH	2.09	50	.04
BHL	vs.	WHL	.68	51	.49

Note. [a] Two tailed.

Table 10

Mean Comparison Tests of Significance for Attitudes toward
Different Types of Peers (SemD Data) (n=158)

Comparison			t	df	p^a
BNPH	vs.	WNPH	2.11	51	.04
BPH	vs.	WPH	-.98	50	.33
BHL	vs.	WHL	1.07	51	.29

Note. [a] Two tailed.

(see Table 7). The subjects preferred to associate more closely with WNPH peers ($M = 92.53$, $SD = 19.74$) than BNPH peers ($M = 85.00$, $SD = 25.61$), with WPH peers ($M = 82.41$, $SD = 26.65$) than BPH peers ($M = 76.01$, $SD = 29.17$), and with WHL peers ($M = 66.14$, $SD = 32.26$) than BHL peers ($M = 60.57$, $SD = 32.99$).

In summary, White, housed children in grades six through twelve had significantly more positive attitudes towards NPH peers over PH peers, NPH peers over HL peers, and PH peers over HL peers on two measures of attitudes (ABS and SemD). These subjects also significantly preferred to associate more closely with NPH peers than PH peers, NPH peers than HL peers, and PH peers than HL peers as was hypothesized in hypotheses four, five, and six. Ethnicity was a significant factor on the ABS where the subjects expressed significantly more positive attitudes towards White peers than Black peers, when they were described as nonpoor housed or poor housed. This finding was not replicated when attitudes were measured using the SemD where the subjects were significantly more positive toward White peers than Black peers, only when they were described as nonpoor housed. On neither measure were subjects' attitudes significantly different when comparing White and Black homeless peers. When the subjects' associational preferences were assessed using the SocD, the subjects responded that they preferred to associate significantly more closely with White peers than Black peers across all levels of housing.

IV
Discussion

Introduction

The results of this study demonstrated that nonpoor, housed children in grades six through twelve had more negative attitudes toward their homeless peers than they did toward poor housed peers or nonpoor housed peers and more negative attitudes toward their poor housed peers than they did toward their nonpoor housed peers. These negative attitudes were also reflected in their responses when they were asked with whom they would like to associate. Nonpoor, housed children preferred to associate more closely with nonpoor housed peers than poor housed peers or homeless peers and preferred to associate more closely with poor housed peers than homeless peers. When race of peer was added as a variable, White subjects had more positive attitudes toward White peers than Black peers, when they were described as nonpoor housed, on both measures of attitude, and when they were described as poor housed on one measure of attitude. When asked for associational preferences, the subjects preferred to associate more closely with White peers, regardless of whether they were nonpoor, poor or homeless.

The children in this study may have viewed children from other social classes or ethnicities as out-groups while viewing children of the same social class or ethnicity as in-groups. Sherman (1990) reported that when social groups are formed among children in school, social class and racial prejudice can play an important role. Prejudice encompasses social and psychological phenomena that include stereotyping, conforming, in-group and out-group categorizing, scapegoating, self-fulfilling prophecies, ethnocentrism, and identifying with a group. In-groups, when they exclude some and admit others, lay the foundation for discrimination and prejudice. It is the in-group's views and attitudes that are the standards by which the out-group is judged. They help form the perception that association with out-group individuals may be detrimental to the individual's social standing in the in-group (Byrnes, 1988), thereby discouraging friendships with out-group individuals.

Attitudes and Associational Preferences Toward Peers

Nonpoor housed children had more positive attitudes (as measured by the ABS and SemD) toward, and preferred to associate more closely with (as measured by the SocD), peers who were more like themselves when the differences involved socioeconomic status. Nonpoor housed peers were preferred to poor housed peers (hypotheses 1 and 4) on all measures. The difference between nonpoor housed and poor housed peers is socioeconomic status in addition to any expectations, stereotypes, and prejudices that nonpoor housed children might believe about either group. It is not surprising that middle class children have more positive attitudes toward peers more like themselves than their poorer classmates. Children tend to learn their values, loyalties, and prejudices from their parents (Sherman, 1990) and tend to have them supported and perpetuated by their community (Byrnes, 1988). Most surveys show American adults to be unsupportive of poor people (Toro & McDonell, 1992) or have found negative attitudes toward the poor (Barney, Fredericks, Fredericks, & Robinson, 1985; Apetekar, 1990; Chafel, 1990; Ferguson, 1990). Not only among adults but also among children in school, social class is a significant factor in the formation of in-groups (Glock, as cited in Sherman, 1990).

Homeless peers are distinguished from nonpoor housed peers not only by socioeconomic status but also level of housing. Both poor housed and homeless children are poor but, homeless children have no permanent residence in addition to being poor. When the attitudes and associational preferences of nonpoor housed children toward homeless peers (hypotheses 2 and 5) were compared to their attitudes and associational preferences toward nonpoor housed peers the children were again more positive towards and preferred to associate more closely with the group that was more nearly like themselves (nonpoor housed). In addition to all of the studies that found negative attitudes toward the poor (e.g., Barney, Fredericks, Fredericks, & Robinson, 1985), many studies have found negative attitudes toward homeless people. For example, Rafferty and Rollins (1989a) discussed at length how homeless children felt picked on in school. They also reported in another study (1989b) that homeless children tended to be more shy and withdrawn, making it more difficult to make friends and engender positive feelings on the part of their housed schoolmates. Stronge and Tenhouse (1990) also reported that homeless children are often stigmatized by their schoolmates, while others found that the stigmatization serves to isolate homeless children as an out-group (Whitman, Accardo, Boyert, & Kendagor, 1990).

Teacher attitudes can have a significant effect on how a student performs or is treated in school. Jacobs (1978) found that teachers in general hold prejudices against certain kinds of students and simply labeling a student can result in differential treatment (Sutherland & Algozzine, 1979). Teachers are influenced by these expectations and preconceptions. They treat students differently according to them, giving more educational opportunities to certain groups thereby changing their behavior and how they are viewed by their peers (Richey & Ysseldyke, 1983).

When nonpoor housed children were asked their attitudes and associational preferences (hypotheses 3 and 6) based only upon level of housing status (poor housed vs. homeless) they again were significantly more positive towards peers more like themselves. They had significantly more positive attitudes toward poor housed peers than homeless peers. Many studies have found that growing up in poverty is a key contributor to a variety of problems (e.g., Chafel, 1990). When matched groups of poor and homeless children were compared, both groups evidenced problems. These problems included developmental delays, psychological and emotional problems, poor school performance, and a variety of health problems (Bassuk & Rosenberg, 1988; Marcus et al. 1991; Rescola, Parker, Stolley, 1991). These findings suggest that there is little difference between the two groups but, Rafferty and Shinn (1991) in their recent survey of the literature comparing poor and homeless children concluded that although there are many areas of similarity, in both health and education homeless children are clearly at greater risk for more health problems and greater difficulty in school than poor housed children. Perhaps this greater risk for problems along with the stereotyping homeless children face in school, combined to make them "more" of an out-group than poor children, and this is why nonpoor children had more negative attitudes toward homeless children than children who were just poor. Nonpoor housed peers (in-group) were preferred to poor housed (out-group) or homeless children (out-group) and poor housed children were preferred to homeless children. Therefore, there was a more negative attitude and less desire to associate with homeless children than any other group, making them an even less desirable out-group.

Ethnicity of Peer As a Factor

This study also investigated how ethnicity of peer would affect the attitudes and associational preferences of White nonpoor housed children. Applying in-group, out-group theory as it was applied above would lead to expectations that again the children would express more positive attitudes and prefer to associate more closely with White peers than Black peers across all levels of socioeconomic status (White nonpoor housed over Black nonpoor housed, White poor housed over Black poor housed, and White homeless over Black homeless), regardless of the measure (ABS, SemD, or SocD) of attitudes or associational preference. The results indicate that this was not always the case. Even when mean score differences were significant in the direction expected, there was much disagreement among the individual respondents. For example, when attitudes were measured by the ABS (see Table 5), the standard deviation was almost twice as great for Black nonpoor housed peers (SD = 19.55) as for White nonpoor housed peers (SD = 10.23) and was almost 50% greater for Black homeless peers (SD = 24.01) than for White homeless peers (SD = 16.82).

When attitudes were measured by the ABS, ethnicity was found to be a significant factor (see Tables 2 and 9). More positive attitudes were expressed toward White peers than Black peers when they were described as nonpoor or poor but, not when they were described as homeless. Similarly, when associational preferences were measured by the SocD, the subjects significantly preferred to associate more closely with White peers than Black peers (see Table 7) across all levels of housing. This finding is not surprising considering that Thomas and Lee (1990) found ethnicity to be a significant factor in the rating of students by their fellow students. In terms of in-group, out-group theory, a survey of 3,500 high school students in Michigan, reported that the separation of different ethnic groups was found to be a natural occurrence (Polakow-Suransky & Ulaby, 1990) with the same ethnicity being an in-group and other ethnicities being out-groups. In addition, the amount of racism and prejudice currently reported in our secondary school system (Pine & Hilliard, 1990; Polakow-Suransky & Ulaby, 1990) suggests that some students may hold prejudices against minorities and the results obtained here may have reflected those prejudices to some degree.

When attitudes were measured by the SemD, there was no main effect for ethnicity (see Table 3). As can be seen from Table 9, White nonpoor housed children expressed significantly more positive attitudes toward White nonpoor housed peers than Black nonpoor housed peers but, this was the only comparison pair where the difference between the means was significant. Neither poor housed nor homeless peer mean attitude score differences were significant when compared by ethnicity. The difference in attitudes between the ABS and SemD is probably because although these instruments measure the same construct, they are not identical and measure the construct differently. The ABS is a more direct measure of attitude. The SemD has been reported to be a more affective measure by some researchers, evoking more of an emotional response (Henerson, Morris, & Fitz-Gibbon, 1987). Others report using the SemD as a multidimensional measure of the attitude itself, as well as the strength of the attitude that can vary considerably depending on the concept being judged (Pedhazur & Schmelkin, 1991).

Summarizing, on both measures the subjects had more negative attitudes toward Black, nonpoor, housed peers than White, nonpoor, housed peers and their associational preferences reflected this. They were divided when comparing Black, poor, housed peers to White, poor, housed peers in that on one measure their attitudes were more negative toward Blacks (ABS) while on the other measure the difference was not significant, but their associational preference was significantly more negative toward Blacks. When asked to rate homeless peers, there was no significant difference on either measure of attitude when the peer was described as either Black or White but, they still preferred to associate significantly more closely with White homeless peers than Black. Further, there was much disagreement and variability between the individual respondents on both the ABS and the SemD when it came to ethnicity.

The amount of variability between individual respondents can be seen by comparing standard deviations for the various treatment groups. When attitudes were measured by the ABS (see Table 5), the standard deviation was almost twice as great for Black nonpoor housed peers (SD = 19.55) as for White nonpoor housed peers (SD = 10.23) and was almost 50% greater for Black homeless peers (SD = 24.01) than for White homeless peers (SD = 16.82). A similar pattern emerged with the SemD data (see Table 6) but to a slightly lesser degree. Here the difference in variability ranged from 27% (Black poor housed peers vs. White poor housed peers) to 44% (Black homeless peers vs. White homeless peers) but, in every case, there was more variability when the subjects rated a Black peer than a White peer across all three levels of socioeconomic status. Some of the variability may be explained by looking at a frequency distribution of the scores (see Appendices I and J) on the ABS. The data for Black, nonpoor, housed peers has an outlier, while the Black homeless data appears to be bimodal. The White nonpoor, housed data has a much tighter grouping and appears skewed. On the SemD, all the distributions for White peers appear to simulate normal distributions (the White homeless data has an outlier) while the Black nonpoor, housed and Black homeless data appear bimodal. Subjecting the data on both these measures to a test of homogeneity of variance (see Appendix K) reveals that the ABS data violates the assumption of homogeneity for both race and SES (levels of housing), while the SemD data does not. A violation of homogeneity means that extreme caution must be exercised when generalizing from these results. In this study the violation is less critical only because the groups have almost equal numbers of subjects and may have several explanations which are discussed below.

The reason for the greater disagreement when White subjects were asked for their attitudes toward Black peers than White peers may be explained in a variety of ways. Discriminatory behavior often surfaces, *not* when a behavior will look prejudicial, but when it can safely hide behind some other motive (Myers, 1990). The subjects in this study may have responded in a manner which they felt was socially desirable rather than in a manner that indicated their true beliefs. This type of response bias may have occurred even though the subjects were assured that their responses would be kept in confidence. They may have varied in the degree to which they felt safe about expressing their true feelings on measures such as the ones used here, and being asked to respond in their school setting. This study was group administered and may have yielded different results if the children responded in a milieu where they felt more secure in their anonymity. Future researchers may need to do more to insure this. Further, Muir, (1989) in surveys conducted over 25 years on attitudes of Whites toward Blacks at the university level, reported that he, too, had found extensive variability in attitudes from year to year. Toro and McDonell (1992) also reported extensive variability in their survey of attitudes toward poor and homeless people particularly in attitudes toward Black homeless people and found that their subjects (adults in the Buffalo area) tended to be less positive toward poor people than homeless people. This variability may best be explained by contact theory described by Allport (1954, as cited in Damico, Bell-Nathaniel, & Green, 1981) and as applied to the educational system by Cohen (1975, as cited in Damico, Bell-Nathaniel, & Green, 1981).

According to contact theory, it is the nature and extent of contact with Black people that determines the attitudes of White people (Damico, Bell-Nathaniel, & Green, 1981). Byrnes (1988) believes that television and films abound with stereotypical portrayals of certain groups and in some cases may be a child's only exposure to those groups. The children in this study reside in a predominantly White suburb and may have had infrequent contact with minorities or their contact may have been quite limited in terms of the different roles in which they encountered minorities. Variations in the quality and frequency of contact that the children in this study have had with Black people may account for the wide spread of attitudes found in the current study. This is supported by findings that suggest that White subjects who were well acquainted with Black people reported they were more comfortable in their experiences with Black people than were subjects who had had a moderate amount of contact with them (Claney & Parker, 1989). Other studies have found variations in the attitudes of White subjects toward Black people depended on the number of Black friends the White subjects reported having (Damico, Bell-Nathaniel, & Green, 1981).

In this study, contact with homeless people was directly controlled for, while contact with Black people was not. Randomization in sampling and assignment to treatment group was the only way in which control was attempted. Although not anticipated, it is not surprising that there was so much variation, that it occurred across different levels of socioeconomic status, and that it occurred on different measures. Future research should control more directly for this by asking the subjects to report their frequency of contact with minorities and should also ask the subjects to at least rate the quality of that contact.

In addition, this study only involved grades six through twelve, in one suburban school district, and was restricted to White nonpoor housed subjects, therefore, it has limited ability to be generalized to other populations. Future investigation is needed to see if these results can be replicated in other grades as well as in other suburban areas. Further study is also needed to see if minority students also hold negative attitudes toward their homeless peers and to see if any of the results can be replicated in both urban and rural areas.

Anecdotal material has reported that homeless children feel stigmatized when they attend school (e.g., Rafferty & Rollins, 1989a) but this perception has not been part of a controlled study. The role of perceived acceptance as it relates to school success needs to be placed in proper perspective among all the factors that impact on school success. Controlled outcome studies are needed to determine if any interventions are effective in changing attitudes or promoting acceptance. If positive results are found, perhaps these interventions could then be used more broadly to change attitudes toward other out-groups both in school and out.

In conclusion, this study suggests that when homeless children attend school their peers in school have negative attitudes toward them, and prefer not to associate with them, because they are poor and homeless. These negative attitudes and associational preferences can become even stronger if the child is from an ethnic minority. Negative attitudes make it more difficult for the homeless children to feel accepted in school and make it more difficult for them to make friends. When children do not feel welcomed in school they may be at greater risk not to attend regularly, to get lower grades, to repeat a grade, and to eventually drop out of school.

Implications of the Study

Homeless children are at high risk to not perform well in school. For example, homeless children have poor attendance records and when they do attend school, they score lower on standardized tests, have a greater risk of repeating a grade, and have a higher rate of dropping out than do other groups including other poor children (e.g., Rafferty & Rollins, 1989a). They also have difficulty making and keeping friends in school (e.g., Eddowes & Hranitz, 1989). Aside from all the difficulties homeless children have that are related to poverty and the lack of a permanent residence, the State of New Jersey recognized how important socialization was to school success when it recommended in its education action plan for homeless children that the school districts ensure that homeless students are absorbed into the mainstream of school life (Doolan, Georgedes, Dillman, & Willis, 1989).

This study suggests that when homeless students are enrolled in school, a negative attitude may exist among many of the students who will be their classmates and these students may prefer not to associate and become friends with these homeless students. If these children then feel unwanted, or as if they do not belong, or are outcasts, the situation can then become a precursor of school failure regardless of what other problems the homeless children might bring with them to school. Schools must attend to the social and psychological well being of homeless students if they expect the students to be successful (Stronge & Tenhouse, 1990). The classmates of the homeless students should be encouraged to have a positive attitude which welcomes them to the class, helps them feel they belong and builds their self esteem.

Contact theory can then be applied to the school and classroom for the purpose of improving the acceptance of homeless students by their classmates when enrolling in new classes. Hartup (1989) found that a child's effectiveness in dealing with the social world emerges largely from experience in close relationships. In early adolescence self esteem may be at its lowest, but self esteem is very important in dealing with a social world such as a school or classroom. Being made to feel you are part of a group such as a new class, is a great enhancer of self esteem (Searcy, 1988). Several studies have reported how skills training programs can be used to change the behavior of children in out-groups, such as homeless children, to improve the quality of contact when contact occurs and thereby change the attitudes of in-group children.

There have been several programs that have worked with problem children and have gotten positive results. These programs might also work with homeless children to improve their chances of being accepted, making friends, and being successful in school. Bretzing and Caterino (1984) got positive results using group counseling with a variety of students who had poor peer relationships, behavior problems, poor self concepts, bad attitudes toward school, and tended to be withdrawn. A life skills training program got excellent results with minority homeless adolescents by developing the skills of the individual participants and creating meaningful roles for them in the environment (Dusenbury, Botvin, & James-Ortiz, 1989). Stewart (1988) worked with in-group students and found that there was a significant positive improvement in their attitudes when they participated in a weight training program with disabled students. Walsh and Buckley (1994) felt that educating the children and staff improved the school environment significantly. Gonzalez (1990) reported on a program for homeless students in Dallas, Texas. The orientation of this program was to make the students feel accepted by both peers and staff at school. They assigned "special friends" to the homeless students to assist them and provided a warm reception and sense of belonging. The program was selected as an exemplary program for how to provide educational services to homeless children. While in Seattle the KOOL-IS (Kids Organized on Learning in School) program tries to create a safe environment within the school that homeless children can turn to whenever they need to (James, Smith & Mann, 1991).

The problems of homeless children and their families are an important challenge for this country. Homelessness is a growing problem and must be addressed before it becomes generational. A scientific approach to the problems homeless children face in school, which builds on current knowledge, gathers further information, attempts solutions in an organized way, and measures and evaluates outcomes is the only sensible way to proceed to solve these problems. This study suggests that children in school have negative attitudes toward homeless children which the homeless children must face when they come to school. If future study shows that these negative attitudes are widely held and if it is determined that these negative attitudes are an impediment to a successful school experience for homeless children, then programs such as those suggested above should be implemented to see if they can change attitudes and give homeless children a better chance to succeed.

Appendix A

ATTITUDE AND BELIEF SCALE I

Directions:

First write the information about yourself below. Then turn the page.

_____ Male _____ Female

Grade_____ Age_____ Birthdate_____

School_____

Ethnicity_____

Have you ever been homeless?   ___Y ___N

Has a member of your family ever been homeless?   ___Y ___N

Who?_____

Do you know anyone who has ever been homeless?   ___Y ___N

Who?_____

Do your parents own the home in which you live?   ___Y ___N

Do your parents rent the home in which you live?   ___Y ___N

Read each statement and indicate with a circle the degree to which you agree or disagree with the statement.

1. Most homeless White students require close supervision.

DISAGREE	DISAGREE	DISAGREE	AGREE	AGREE	AGREE
STRONGLY	SOMEWHAT	SLIGHTLY	SLIGHTLY	SOMEWHAT	STRONGLY

2. Homeless White students try to manipulate their helpers.

DISAGREE	DISAGREE	DISAGREE	AGREE	AGREE	AGREE
STRONGLY	SOMEWHAT	SLIGHTLY	SLIGHTLY	SOMEWHAT	STRONGLY

3. Homeless White students are more dangerous than other people.

DISAGREE	DISAGREE	DISAGREE	AGREE	AGREE	AGREE
STRONGLY	SOMEWHAT	SLIGHTLY	SLIGHTLY	SOMEWHAT	STRONGLY

4. Homeless White students do poorly in school.

DISAGREE	DISAGREE	DISAGREE	AGREE	AGREE	AGREE
STRONGLY	SOMEWHAT	SLIGHTLY	SLIGHTLY	SOMEWHAT	STRONGLY

5. Many White people are homeless because they lost their homes by eviction or foreclosure.

DISAGREE	DISAGREE	DISAGREE	AGREE	AGREE	AGREE
STRONGLY	SOMEWHAT	SLIGHTLY	SLIGHTLY	SOMEWHAT	STRONGLY

6. I cross the street to avoid homeless White people.

DISAGREE	DISAGREE	DISAGREE	AGREE	AGREE	AGREE
STRONGLY	SOMEWHAT	SLIGHTLY	SLIGHTLY	SOMEWHAT	STRONGLY

7. Homeless White students listen to their teachers.

| DISAGREE | DISAGREE | DISAGREE | AGREE | AGREE | AGREE |
| STRONGLY | SOMEWHAT | SLIGHTLY | SLIGHTLY | SOMEWHAT | STRONGLY |

8. It is unsafe to allow homeless White people to gather in public places.

| DISAGREE | DISAGREE | DISAGREE | AGREE | AGREE | AGREE |
| STRONGLY | SOMEWHAT | SLIGHTLY | SLIGHTLY | SOMEWHAT | STRONGLY |

9. The more homeless White people there are in a neighborhood, the more dangerous that neighborhood becomes.

| DISAGREE | DISAGREE | DISAGREE | AGREE | AGREE | AGREE |
| STRONGLY | SOMEWHAT | SLIGHTLY | SLIGHTLY | SOMEWHAT | STRONGLY |

10. Homelessness is largely the result of our economic system.

| DISAGREE | DISAGREE | DISAGREE | AGREE | AGREE | AGREE |
| STRONGLY | SOMEWHAT | SLIGHTLY | SLIGHTLY | SOMEWHAT | STRONGLY |

11. Society and government are more responsible for more homelessness than homeless White people.

| DISAGREE | DISAGREE | DISAGREE | AGREE | AGREE | AGREE |
| STRONGLY | SOMEWHAT | SLIGHTLY | SLIGHTLY | SOMEWHAT | STRONGLY |

12. I would not be willing to work on a group project in school with a homeless White student.

| DISAGREE | DISAGREE | DISAGREE | AGREE | AGREE | AGREE |
| STRONGLY | SOMEWHAT | SLIGHTLY | SLIGHTLY | SOMEWHAT | STRONGLY |

13. If homeless White people learn appropriate skills, they could improve their situation.

DISAGREE	DISAGREE	DISAGREE	AGREE	AGREE	AGREE
STRONGLY	SOMEWHAT	SLIGHTLY	SLIGHTLY	SOMEWHAT	STRONGLY

14. Homeless White students are responsible enough to do their homework and study for tests.

DISAGREE	DISAGREE	DISAGREE	AGREE	AGREE	AGREE
STRONGLY	SOMEWHAT	SLIGHTLY	SLIGHTLY	SOMEWHAT	STRONGLY

15. Homeless White students are motivated to do well in school.

DISAGREE	DISAGREE	DISAGREE	AGREE	AGREE	AGREE
STRONGLY	SOMEWHAT	SLIGHTLY	SLIGHTLY	SOMEWHAT	STRONGLY

16. Most homeless White people have chosen to be homeless.

DISAGREE	DISAGREE	DISAGREE	AGREE	AGREE	AGREE
STRONGLY	SOMEWHAT	SLIGHTLY	SLIGHTLY	SOMEWHAT	STRONGLY

17. Even if homeless White people behave well, it is dangerous to forget that they are homeless.

DISAGREE	DISAGREE	DISAGREE	AGREE	AGREE	AGREE
STRONGLY	SOMEWHAT	SLIGHTLY	SLIGHTLY	SOMEWHAT	STRONGLY

18. I would write a letter to my Congressman stating my support for programs serving homeless White persons.

DISAGREE	DISAGREE	DISAGREE	AGREE	AGREE	AGREE
STRONGLY	SOMEWHAT	SLIGHTLY	SLIGHTLY	SOMEWHAT	STRONGLY

19. Most homeless White people could take care of themselves if given the opportunity.

DISAGREE   DISAGREE   DISAGREE   AGREE   AGREE   AGREE
STRONGLY   SOMEWHAT   SLIGHTLY   SLIGHTLY   SOMEWHAT   STRONGLY

20. Homeless White people cannot be trusted.

DISAGREE   DISAGREE   DISAGREE   AGREE   AGREE   AGREE
STRONGLY   SOMEWHAT   SLIGHTLY   SLIGHTLY   SOMEWHAT   STRONGLY

21. You cannot tell what homeless White people are going to do from one minute to the next.

DISAGREE   DISAGREE   DISAGREE   AGREE   AGREE   AGREE
STRONGLY   SOMEWHAT   SLIGHTLY   SLIGHTLY   SOMEWHAT   STRONGLY

22. I would not be frightened to have a shelter for homeless White people located near my home.

DISAGREE   DISAGREE   DISAGREE   AGREE   AGREE   AGREE
STRONGLY   SOMEWHAT   SLIGHTLY   SLIGHTLY   SOMEWHAT   STRONGLY

23. Homeless White students are responsible for doing poorly in school.

DISAGREE   DISAGREE   DISAGREE   AGREE   AGREE   AGREE
STRONGLY   SOMEWHAT   SLIGHTLY   SLIGHTLY   SOMEWHAT   STRONGLY

24. Homeless White people are more likely to commit violent crimes than other people.

DISAGREE   DISAGREE   DISAGREE   AGREE   AGREE   AGREE
STRONGLY   SOMEWHAT   SLIGHTLY   SLIGHTLY   SOMEWHAT   STRONGLY

25. I would be willing to volunteer some time tutoring a homeless White student.

DISAGREE   DISAGREE   DISAGREE   AGREE   AGREE   AGREE
STRONGLY   SOMEWHAT   SLIGHTLY   SLIGHTLY SOMEWHAT STRONGLY

26. Homeless White people are resistant to the help offered to them.

DISAGREE   DISAGREE   DISAGREE   AGREE   AGREE   AGREE
STRONGLY   SOMEWHAT   SLIGHTLY   SLIGHTLY SOMEWHAT STRONGLY

27. I would be willing to pay more in taxes in order to help homeless White people.

DISAGREE   DISAGREE   DISAGREE   AGREE   AGREE   AGREE
STRONGLY   SOMEWHAT   SLIGHTLY   SLIGHTLY SOMEWHAT STRONGLY

28. Most people are afraid of homeless White people.

DISAGREE   DISAGREE   DISAGREE   AGREE   AGREE   AGREE
STRONGLY   SOMEWHAT   SLIGHTLY   SLIGHTLY SOMEWHAT STRONGLY

ATTITUDE AND BELIEF SCALE II

Directions:

First write the information about yourself below. Then turn the page.

_____ Male _____Female

Grade_____ Age_____ Birthdate_____

School_____

Ethnicity_____

Have you ever been homeless?   ___Y ___N

Has a member of your family ever been homeless?   ___Y ___N

Who?_____

Do you know anyone who has ever been homeless?   ___Y ___N

Who?_____

Do your parents own the home in which you live?   ___Y ___N

Do your parents rent the home in which you live?   ___Y ___N

Read each statement and indicate with a circle the degree to which you agree or disagree with the statement.

1. Most homeless Black students require close supervision.

DISAGREE	DISAGREE	DISAGREE	AGREE	AGREE	AGREE
STRONGLY	SOMEWHAT	SLIGHTLY	SLIGHTLY	SOMEWHAT	STRONGLY

2. Homeless Black students try to manipulate their helpers.

DISAGREE	DISAGREE	DISAGREE	AGREE	AGREE	AGREE
STRONGLY	SOMEWHAT	SLIGHTLY	SLIGHTLY	SOMEWHAT	STRONGLY

3. Homeless Black students are more dangerous than other people.

DISAGREE	DISAGREE	DISAGREE	AGREE	AGREE	AGREE
STRONGLY	SOMEWHAT	SLIGHTLY	SLIGHTLY	SOMEWHAT	STRONGLY

4. Homeless Black students do poorly in school.

DISAGREE	DISAGREE	DISAGREE	AGREE	AGREE	AGREE
STRONGLY	SOMEWHAT	SLIGHTLY	SLIGHTLY	SOMEWHAT	STRONGLY

5. Many Black people are homeless because they lost their homes by eviction or foreclosure.

DISAGREE	DISAGREE	DISAGREE	AGREE	AGREE	AGREE
STRONGLY	SOMEWHAT	SLIGHTLY	SLIGHTLY	SOMEWHAT	STRONGLY

6. I cross the street to avoid homeless Black people.

DISAGREE	DISAGREE	DISAGREE	AGREE	AGREE	AGREE
STRONGLY	SOMEWHAT	SLIGHTLY	SLIGHTLY	SOMEWHAT	STRONGLY

7. Homeless Black students listen to their teachers.

DISAGREE   DISAGREE   DISAGREE   AGREE   AGREE   AGREE
STRONGLY   SOMEWHAT   SLIGHTLY   SLIGHTLY   SOMEWHAT   STRONGLY

8. It is unsafe to allow homeless Black people to gather in public places.

DISAGREE   DISAGREE   DISAGREE   AGREE   AGREE   AGREE
STRONGLY   SOMEWHAT   SLIGHTLY   SLIGHTLY   SOMEWHAT   STRONGLY

9. The more homeless Black people there are in a neighborhood, the more dangerous that neighborhood becomes.

DISAGREE   DISAGREE   DISAGREE   AGREE   AGREE   AGREE
STRONGLY   SOMEWHAT   SLIGHTLY   SLIGHTLY   SOMEWHAT   STRONGLY

10. Homelessness is largely the result of our economic system.

DISAGREE   DISAGREE   DISAGREE   AGREE   AGREE   AGREE
STRONGLY   SOMEWHAT   SLIGHTLY   SLIGHTLY   SOMEWHAT   STRONGLY

11. Society and government are more responsible for more homelessness than homeless Black people.

DISAGREE   DISAGREE   DISAGREE   AGREE   AGREE   AGREE
STRONGLY   SOMEWHAT   SLIGHTLY   SLIGHTLY   SOMEWHAT   STRONGLY

12. I would not be willing to work on a group project in school with a homeless Black student.

DISAGREE   DISAGREE   DISAGREE   AGREE   AGREE   AGREE
STRONGLY   SOMEWHAT   SLIGHTLY   SLIGHTLY   SOMEWHAT   STRONGLY

13. If homeless Black people learn appropriate skills, they could improve their situation.

DISAGREE   DISAGREE   DISAGREE   AGREE   AGREE   AGREE
STRONGLY   SOMEWHAT   SLIGHTLY   SLIGHTLY   SOMEWHAT   STRONGLY

14. Homeless Black students are responsible enough to do their homework and study for tests.

DISAGREE   DISAGREE   DISAGREE   AGREE   AGREE   AGREE
STRONGLY   SOMEWHAT   SLIGHTLY   SLIGHTLY   SOMEWHAT   STRONGLY

15. Homeless Black students are motivated to do well in school.

DISAGREE   DISAGREE   DISAGREE   AGREE   AGREE   AGREE
STRONGLY   SOMEWHAT   SLIGHTLY   SLIGHTLY   SOMEWHAT   STRONGLY

16. Most homeless Black people have chosen to be homeless.

DISAGREE   DISAGREE   DISAGREE   AGREE   AGREE   AGREE
STRONGLY   SOMEWHAT   SLIGHTLY   SLIGHTLY   SOMEWHAT   STRONGLY

17. Even if homeless Black people behave well, it is dangerous to forget that they are homeless.

DISAGREE   DISAGREE   DISAGREE   AGREE   AGREE   AGREE
STRONGLY   SOMEWHAT   SLIGHTLY   SLIGHTLY   SOMEWHAT   STRONGLY

18. I would write a letter to my Congressman stating my support for programs serving homeless Black persons.

DISAGREE   DISAGREE   DISAGREE   AGREE   AGREE   AGREE
STRONGLY   SOMEWHAT   SLIGHTLY   SLIGHTLY   SOMEWHAT   STRONGLY

19. Most homeless Black people could take care of themselves if given the opportunity.

DISAGREE   DISAGREE   DISAGREE   AGREE   AGREE   AGREE
STRONGLY   SOMEWHAT   SLIGHTLY   SLIGHTLY   SOMEWHAT   STRONGLY

20. Homeless Black people cannot be trusted.

DISAGREE   DISAGREE   DISAGREE   AGREE   AGREE   AGREE
STRONGLY   SOMEWHAT   SLIGHTLY   SLIGHTLY   SOMEWHAT   STRONGLY

21. You cannot tell what homeless Black people are going to do from one minute to the next.

DISAGREE   DISAGREE   DISAGREE   AGREE   AGREE   AGREE
STRONGLY   SOMEWHAT   SLIGHTLY   SLIGHTLY   SOMEWHAT   STRONGLY

22. I would not be frightened to have a shelter for homeless Black people located near my home.

DISAGREE   DISAGREE   DISAGREE   AGREE   AGREE   AGREE
STRONGLY   SOMEWHAT   SLIGHTLY   SLIGHTLY   SOMEWHAT   STRONGLY

23. Homeless Black students are responsible for doing poorly in school.

DISAGREE   DISAGREE   DISAGREE   AGREE   AGREE   AGREE
STRONGLY   SOMEWHAT   SLIGHTLY   SLIGHTLY   SOMEWHAT   STRONGLY

24. Homeless Black people are more likely to commit violent crimes than other people.

DISAGREE   DISAGREE   DISAGREE   AGREE   AGREE   AGREE
STRONGLY   SOMEWHAT   SLIGHTLY   SLIGHTLY   SOMEWHAT   STRONGLY

25. I would be willing to volunteer some time tutoring a homeless Black student.

DISAGREE   DISAGREE   DISAGREE   AGREE   AGREE   AGREE
STRONGLY   SOMEWHAT   SLIGHTLY   SLIGHTLY   SOMEWHAT   STRONGLY

26. Homeless Black people are resistant to the help offered to them.

DISAGREE   DISAGREE   DISAGREE   AGREE   AGREE   AGREE
STRONGLY   SOMEWHAT   SLIGHTLY   SLIGHTLY   SOMEWHAT   STRONGLY

27. I would be willing to pay more in taxes in order to help homeless Black people.

DISAGREE   DISAGREE   DISAGREE   AGREE   AGREE   AGREE
STRONGLY   SOMEWHAT   SLIGHTLY   SLIGHTLY   SOMEWHAT   STRONGLY

28. Most people are afraid of homeless Black people.

DISAGREE   DISAGREE   DISAGREE   AGREE   AGREE   AGREE
STRONGLY   SOMEWHAT   SLIGHTLY   SLIGHTLY   SOMEWHAT   STRONGLY

ATTITUDE AND BELIEF SCALE III

Directions:

First write the information about yourself below. Then turn the page.

_____ Male _____Female

Grade_____   Age_____   Birthdate_____

School_____

Ethnicity_____

Have you ever been homeless?   ___Y ___N

Has a member of your family ever been homeless?   ___Y ___N

Who?_____

Do you know anyone who has ever been homeless?   ___Y ___N

Who?_____

Do your parents own the home in which you live?   ___Y ___N

Do your parents rent the home in which you live?   ___Y ___N

Read each statement and indicate with a circle the degree to which you agree or disagree with the statement.

1. Most poor White students require close supervision.

| DISAGREE | DISAGREE | DISAGREE | AGREE | AGREE | AGREE |
| STRONGLY | SOMEWHAT | SLIGHTLY | SLIGHTLY | SOMEWHAT | STRONGLY |

2. Poor White students try to manipulate their helpers.

| DISAGREE | DISAGREE | DISAGREE | AGREE | AGREE | AGREE |
| STRONGLY | SOMEWHAT | SLIGHTLY | SLIGHTLY | SOMEWHAT | STRONGLY |

3. Poor White students are more dangerous than other people.

| DISAGREE | DISAGREE | DISAGREE | AGREE | AGREE | AGREE |
| STRONGLY | SOMEWHAT | SLIGHTLY | SLIGHTLY | SOMEWHAT | STRONGLY |

4. Poor White students do poorly in school.

| DISAGREE | DISAGREE | DISAGREE | AGREE | AGREE | AGREE |
| STRONGLY | SOMEWHAT | SLIGHTLY | SLIGHTLY | SOMEWHAT | STRONGLY |

5. Many White people are poor because they lost their homes by eviction or foreclosure.

| DISAGREE | DISAGREE | DISAGREE | AGREE | AGREE | AGREE |
| STRONGLY | SOMEWHAT | SLIGHTLY | SLIGHTLY | SOMEWHAT | STRONGLY |

6. I cross the street to avoid poor White people.

| DISAGREE | DISAGREE | DISAGREE | AGREE | AGREE | AGREE |
| STRONGLY | SOMEWHAT | SLIGHTLY | SLIGHTLY | SOMEWHAT | STRONGLY |

7. Poor White students listen to their teachers.

DISAGREE   DISAGREE   DISAGREE   AGREE   AGREE   AGREE
STRONGLY   SOMEWHAT   SLIGHTLY   SLIGHTLY   SOMEWHAT   STRONGLY

8. It is unsafe to allow poor White people to gather in public places.

DISAGREE   DISAGREE   DISAGREE   AGREE   AGREE   AGREE
STRONGLY   SOMEWHAT   SLIGHTLY   SLIGHTLY   SOMEWHAT   STRONGLY

9. The more poor White people there are in a neighborhood, the more dangerous that neighborhood becomes.

DISAGREE   DISAGREE   DISAGREE   AGREE   AGREE   AGREE
STRONGLY   SOMEWHAT   SLIGHTLY   SLIGHTLY   SOMEWHAT   STRONGLY

10. Poverty is largely the result of our economic system.

DISAGREE   DISAGREE   DISAGREE   AGREE   AGREE   AGREE
STRONGLY   SOMEWHAT   SLIGHTLY   SLIGHTLY   SOMEWHAT   STRONGLY

11. Society and government are more responsible for more poverty than poor White people.

DISAGREE   DISAGREE   DISAGREE   AGREE   AGREE   AGREE
STRONGLY   SOMEWHAT   SLIGHTLY   SLIGHTLY   SOMEWHAT   STRONGLY

12. I would not be willing to work on a group project in school with a poor White student.

DISAGREE   DISAGREE   DISAGREE   AGREE   AGREE   AGREE
STRONGLY   SOMEWHAT   SLIGHTLY   SLIGHTLY   SOMEWHAT   STRONGLY

13. If poor White people learn appropriate skills, they could improve their situation.

DISAGREE   DISAGREE   DISAGREE   AGREE   AGREE   AGREE
STRONGLY   SOMEWHAT   SLIGHTLY   SLIGHTLY SOMEWHAT   STRONGLY

14. Poor White students are responsible enough to do their homework and study for tests.

DISAGREE   DISAGREE   DISAGREE   AGREE   AGREE   AGREE
STRONGLY   SOMEWHAT   SLIGHTLY   SLIGHTLY SOMEWHAT   STRONGLY

15. Poor White students are motivated to do well in school.

DISAGREE   DISAGREE   DISAGREE   AGREE   AGREE   AGREE
STRONGLY   SOMEWHAT   SLIGHTLY   SLIGHTLY SOMEWHAT   STRONGLY

16. Most poor White people have chosen to be poor.

DISAGREE   DISAGREE   DISAGREE   AGREE   AGREE   AGREE
STRONGLY   SOMEWHAT   SLIGHTLY   SLIGHTLY SOMEWHAT   STRONGLY

17. Even if poor White people behave well, it is dangerous to forget that they are poor.

DISAGREE   DISAGREE   DISAGREE   AGREE   AGREE   AGREE
STRONGLY   SOMEWHAT   SLIGHTLY   SLIGHTLY SOMEWHAT   STRONGLY

18. I would write a letter to my Congressman stating my support for programs serving poor White persons.

DISAGREE   DISAGREE   DISAGREE   AGREE   AGREE   AGREE
STRONGLY   SOMEWHAT   SLIGHTLY   SLIGHTLY SOMEWHAT   STRONGLY

19. Most poor White people could take care of themselves if given the opportunity.

DISAGREE   DISAGREE   DISAGREE   AGREE   AGREE   AGREE
STRONGLY   SOMEWHAT   SLIGHTLY   SLIGHTLY   SOMEWHAT   STRONGLY

20. Poor White people cannot be trusted.

DISAGREE   DISAGREE   DISAGREE   AGREE   AGREE   AGREE
STRONGLY   SOMEWHAT   SLIGHTLY   SLIGHTLY   SOMEWHAT   STRONGLY

21. You cannot tell what poor White people are going to do from one minute to the next.

DISAGREE   DISAGREE   DISAGREE   AGREE   AGREE   AGREE
STRONGLY   SOMEWHAT   SLIGHTLY   SLIGHTLY   SOMEWHAT   STRONGLY

22. I would not be frightened to have a shelter for poor White people located near my home.

DISAGREE   DISAGREE   DISAGREE   AGREE   AGREE   AGREE
STRONGLY   SOMEWHAT   SLIGHTLY   SLIGHTLY   SOMEWHAT   STRONGLY

23. Poor White students are responsible for doing poorly in school.

DISAGREE   DISAGREE   DISAGREE   AGREE   AGREE   AGREE
STRONGLY   SOMEWHAT   SLIGHTLY   SLIGHTLY   SOMEWHAT   STRONGLY

24. Poor White people are more likely to commit violent crimes than other people.

DISAGREE   DISAGREE   DISAGREE   AGREE   AGREE   AGREE
STRONGLY   SOMEWHAT   SLIGHTLY   SLIGHTLY   SOMEWHAT   STRONGLY

25. I would be willing to volunteer some time tutoring a poor White student.

DISAGREE   DISAGREE   DISAGREE   AGREE   AGREE   AGREE
STRONGLY   SOMEWHAT   SLIGHTLY   SLIGHTLY   SOMEWHAT   STRONGLY

26. Poor White people are resistant to the help offered to them.

DISAGREE   DISAGREE   DISAGREE   AGREE   AGREE   AGREE
STRONGLY   SOMEWHAT   SLIGHTLY   SLIGHTLY   SOMEWHAT   STRONGLY

27. I would be willing to pay more in taxes in order to help poor White people.

DISAGREE   DISAGREE   DISAGREE   AGREE   AGREE   AGREE
STRONGLY   SOMEWHAT   SLIGHTLY   SLIGHTLY   SOMEWHAT   STRONGLY

28. Most people are afraid of poor White people.

DISAGREE   DISAGREE   DISAGREE   AGREE   AGREE   AGREE
STRONGLY   SOMEWHAT   SLIGHTLY   SLIGHTLY   SOMEWHAT   STRONGLY

ATTITUDE AND BELIEF SCALE IV

Directions:

First write the information about yourself below. Then turn the page.

_____ Male _____ Female

Grade_____ Age_____ Birthdate_____

School_____

Ethnicity_____

Have you ever been homeless?   ___Y ___N

Has a member of your family ever been homeless?   ___Y ___N

Who?_____

Do you know anyone who has ever been homeless?   ___Y ___N

Who?_____

Do your parents own the home in which you live?   ___Y ___N

Do your parents rent the home in which you live?   ___Y ___N

Read each statement and indicate with a circle the degree to which you agree or disagree with the statement.

1. Most poor Black students require close supervision.

DISAGREE   DISAGREE   DISAGREE   AGREE   AGREE   AGREE
STRONGLY   SOMEWHAT   SLIGHTLY   SLIGHTLY   SOMEWHAT   STRONGLY

2. Poor Black students try to manipulate their helpers.

DISAGREE   DISAGREE   DISAGREE   AGREE   AGREE   AGREE
STRONGLY   SOMEWHAT   SLIGHTLY   SLIGHTLY   SOMEWHAT   STRONGLY

3. Poor Black students are more dangerous than other people.

DISAGREE   DISAGREE   DISAGREE   AGREE   AGREE   AGREE
STRONGLY   SOMEWHAT   SLIGHTLY   SLIGHTLY   SOMEWHAT   STRONGLY

4. Poor Black students do poorly in school.

DISAGREE   DISAGREE   DISAGREE   AGREE   AGREE   AGREE
STRONGLY   SOMEWHAT   SLIGHTLY   SLIGHTLY   SOMEWHAT   STRONGLY

5. Many Black people are poor because they lost their homes by eviction or foreclosure.

DISAGREE   DISAGREE   DISAGREE   AGREE   AGREE   AGREE
STRONGLY   SOMEWHAT   SLIGHTLY   SLIGHTLY   SOMEWHAT   STRONGLY

6. I cross the street to avoid poor Black people.

DISAGREE   DISAGREE   DISAGREE   AGREE   AGREE   AGREE
STRONGLY   SOMEWHAT   SLIGHTLY   SLIGHTLY   SOMEWHAT   STRONGLY

7. Poor Black students listen to their teachers.

DISAGREE   DISAGREE   DISAGREE   AGREE   AGREE   AGREE
STRONGLY   SOMEWHAT   SLIGHTLY   SLIGHTLY   SOMEWHAT   STRONGLY

8. It is unsafe to allow poor Black people to gather in public places.

DISAGREE   DISAGREE   DISAGREE   AGREE   AGREE   AGREE
STRONGLY   SOMEWHAT   SLIGHTLY   SLIGHTLY   SOMEWHAT   STRONGLY

9. The more poor Black people there are in a neighborhood, the more dangerous that neighborhood becomes.

DISAGREE   DISAGREE   DISAGREE   AGREE   AGREE   AGREE
STRONGLY   SOMEWHAT   SLIGHTLY   SLIGHTLY   SOMEWHAT   STRONGLY

10. Poverty is largely the result of our economic system.

DISAGREE   DISAGREE   DISAGREE   AGREE   AGREE   AGREE
STRONGLY   SOMEWHAT   SLIGHTLY   SLIGHTLY   SOMEWHAT   STRONGLY

11. Society and government are more responsible for most poverty than poor Black people.

DISAGREE   DISAGREE   DISAGREE   AGREE   AGREE   AGREE
STRONGLY   SOMEWHAT   SLIGHTLY   SLIGHTLY   SOMEWHAT   STRONGLY

12. I would not be willing to work on a group project in school with a poor Black student.

DISAGREE   DISAGREE   DISAGREE   AGREE   AGREE   AGREE
STRONGLY   SOMEWHAT   SLIGHTLY   SLIGHTLY   SOMEWHAT   STRONGLY

13. If poor Black people learn appropriate skills, they could improve their situation.

DISAGREE	DISAGREE	DISAGREE	AGREE	AGREE	AGREE
STRONGLY	SOMEWHAT	SLIGHTLY	SLIGHTLY	SOMEWHAT	STRONGLY

14. Poor Black students are responsible enough to do their homework and study for tests.

DISAGREE	DISAGREE	DISAGREE	AGREE	AGREE	AGREE
STRONGLY	SOMEWHAT	SLIGHTLY	SLIGHTLY	SOMEWHAT	STRONGLY

15. Poor Black students are motivated to do well in school.

DISAGREE	DISAGREE	DISAGREE	AGREE	AGREE	AGREE
STRONGLY	SOMEWHAT	SLIGHTLY	SLIGHTLY	SOMEWHAT	STRONGLY

16. Most poor Black people have chosen to be poor.

DISAGREE	DISAGREE	DISAGREE	AGREE	AGREE	AGREE
STRONGLY	SOMEWHAT	SLIGHTLY	SLIGHTLY	SOMEWHAT	STRONGLY

17. Even if poor Black people behave well, it is dangerous to forget that they are poor.

DISAGREE	DISAGREE	DISAGREE	AGREE	AGREE	AGREE
STRONGLY	SOMEWHAT	SLIGHTLY	SLIGHTLY	SOMEWHAT	STRONGLY

18. I would write a letter to my Congressman stating my support for programs serving poor Black persons.

DISAGREE	DISAGREE	DISAGREE	AGREE	AGREE	AGREE
STRONGLY	SOMEWHAT	SLIGHTLY	SLIGHTLY	SOMEWHAT	STRONGLY

19. Most poor Black people could take care of themselves if given the opportunity.

DISAGREE   DISAGREE   DISAGREE   AGREE   AGREE   AGREE
STRONGLY   SOMEWHAT   SLIGHTLY   SLIGHTLY   SOMEWHAT   STRONGLY

20. Poor Black people cannot be trusted.

DISAGREE   DISAGREE   DISAGREE   AGREE   AGREE   AGREE
STRONGLY   SOMEWHAT   SLIGHTLY   SLIGHTLY   SOMEWHAT   STRONGLY

21. You cannot tell what poor Black people are going to do from one minute to the next.

DISAGREE   DISAGREE   DISAGREE   AGREE   AGREE   AGREE
STRONGLY   SOMEWHAT   SLIGHTLY   SLIGHTLY   SOMEWHAT   STRONGLY

22. I would not be frightened to have a shelter for poor Black people located near my home.

DISAGREE   DISAGREE   DISAGREE   AGREE   AGREE   AGREE
STRONGLY   SOMEWHAT   SLIGHTLY   SLIGHTLY   SOMEWHAT   STRONGLY

23. Poor Black students are responsible for doing poorly in school.

DISAGREE   DISAGREE   DISAGREE   AGREE   AGREE   AGREE
STRONGLY   SOMEWHAT   SLIGHTLY   SLIGHTLY   SOMEWHAT   STRONGLY

24. Poor Black people are more likely to commit violent crimes than other people.

DISAGREE   DISAGREE   DISAGREE   AGREE   AGREE   AGREE
STRONGLY   SOMEWHAT   SLIGHTLY   SLIGHTLY   SOMEWHAT   STRONGLY

25. I would be willing to volunteer some time tutoring a poor Black student.

DISAGREE   DISAGREE   DISAGREE   AGREE   AGREE   AGREE
STRONGLY   SOMEWHAT   SLIGHTLY   SLIGHTLY   SOMEWHAT   STRONGLY

26. Poor Black people are resistant to the help offered to them.

DISAGREE   DISAGREE   DISAGREE   AGREE   AGREE   AGREE
STRONGLY   SOMEWHAT   SLIGHTLY   SLIGHTLY   SOMEWHAT   STRONGLY

27. I would be willing to pay more in taxes in order to help poor Black people.

DISAGREE   DISAGREE   DISAGREE   AGREE   AGREE   AGREE
STRONGLY   SOMEWHAT   SLIGHTLY   SLIGHTLY   SOMEWHAT   STRONGLY

28. Most people are afraid of poor Black people.

DISAGREE   DISAGREE   DISAGREE   AGREE   AGREE   AGREE
STRONGLY   SOMEWHAT   SLIGHTLY   SLIGHTLY   SOMEWHAT   STRONGLY

ATTITUDE AND BELIEF SCALE V

Directions:

First write the information about yourself below. Then turn the page.

____ Male ____Female

Grade_____ Age_____ Birthdate_____

School_____

Ethnicity_____

Have you ever been homeless?   ___Y ___N

Has a member of your family ever been homeless?   ___Y ___N

Who?_____

Do you know anyone who has ever been homeless?   ___Y ___N

Who?_____

Do your parents own the home in which you live?   ___Y ___N

Do your parents rent the home in which you live?   ___Y ___N

Read each statement and indicate with a circle the degree to which you agree or disagree with the statement.

1. Most middle class White students require close supervision.

DISAGREE   DISAGREE   DISAGREE   AGREE   AGREE   AGREE
STRONGLY   SOMEWHAT   SLIGHTLY   SLIGHTLY   SOMEWHAT   STRONGLY

2. Middle class White students try to manipulate their helpers.

DISAGREE   DISAGREE   DISAGREE   AGREE   AGREE   AGREE
STRONGLY   SOMEWHAT   SLIGHTLY   SLIGHTLY   SOMEWHAT   STRONGLY

3. Middle class White students are more dangerous than other people.

DISAGREE   DISAGREE   DISAGREE   AGREE   AGREE   AGREE
STRONGLY   SOMEWHAT   SLIGHTLY   SLIGHTLY   SOMEWHAT   STRONGLY

4. Middle class White students do poorly in school.

DISAGREE   DISAGREE   DISAGREE   AGREE   AGREE   AGREE
STRONGLY   SOMEWHAT   SLIGHTLY   SLIGHTLY   SOMEWHAT   STRONGLY

5. Many White people are poor because they lost their homes by eviction or foreclosure.

DISAGREE   DISAGREE   DISAGREE   AGREE   AGREE   AGREE
STRONGLY   SOMEWHAT   SLIGHTLY   SLIGHTLY   SOMEWHAT   STRONGLY

6. I cross the street to avoid middle class White people.

DISAGREE   DISAGREE   DISAGREE   AGREE   AGREE   AGREE
STRONGLY   SOMEWHAT   SLIGHTLY   SLIGHTLY   SOMEWHAT   STRONGLY

7. Middle class White students listen to their teachers.

DISAGREE   DISAGREE   DISAGREE   AGREE   AGREE   AGREE
STRONGLY   SOMEWHAT   SLIGHTLY   SLIGHTLY   SOMEWHAT   STRONGLY

8. It is unsafe to allow middle class White people to gather in public places.

DISAGREE   DISAGREE   DISAGREE   AGREE   AGREE   AGREE
STRONGLY   SOMEWHAT   SLIGHTLY   SLIGHTLY   SOMEWHAT   STRONGLY

9. The more middle class White people there are in a neighborhood, the more dangerous that neighborhood becomes.

DISAGREE   DISAGREE   DISAGREE   AGREE   AGREE   AGREE
STRONGLY   SOMEWHAT   SLIGHTLY   SLIGHTLY   SOMEWHAT   STRONGLY

10. Being middle class is largely the result of our economic system.

DISAGREE   DISAGREE   DISAGREE   AGREE   AGREE   AGREE
STRONGLY   SOMEWHAT   SLIGHTLY   SLIGHTLY   SOMEWHAT   STRONGLY

11. Society and government are more responsible for more poverty than middle class White people.

DISAGREE   DISAGREE   DISAGREE   AGREE   AGREE   AGREE
STRONGLY   SOMEWHAT   SLIGHTLY   SLIGHTLY   SOMEWHAT   STRONGLY

12. I would not be willing to work on a group project in school with a middle class White student.

DISAGREE   DISAGREE   DISAGREE   AGREE   AGREE   AGREE
STRONGLY   SOMEWHAT   SLIGHTLY   SLIGHTLY   SOMEWHAT   STRONGLY

13. If middle class White people learn appropriate skills, they could improve their situation.

DISAGREE   DISAGREE   DISAGREE   AGREE   AGREE   AGREE
STRONGLY   SOMEWHAT   SLIGHTLY   SLIGHTLY   SOMEWHAT   STRONGLY

14. Middle class White students are responsible enough to do their homework and study for tests.

DISAGREE   DISAGREE   DISAGREE   AGREE   AGREE   AGREE
STRONGLY   SOMEWHAT   SLIGHTLY   SLIGHTLY   SOMEWHAT   STRONGLY

15. Middle class White students are motivated to do well in school.

DISAGREE   DISAGREE   DISAGREE   AGREE   AGREE   AGREE
STRONGLY   SOMEWHAT   SLIGHTLY   SLIGHTLY   SOMEWHAT   STRONGLY

16. Most middle class White people have chosen to be middle class.

DISAGREE   DISAGREE   DISAGREE   AGREE   AGREE   AGREE
STRONGLY   SOMEWHAT   SLIGHTLY   SLIGHTLY   SOMEWHAT   STRONGLY

17. Even if middle class White people behave well, it is dangerous to forget that they are middle class.

DISAGREE   DISAGREE   DISAGREE   AGREE   AGREE   AGREE
STRONGLY   SOMEWHAT   SLIGHTLY   SLIGHTLY   SOMEWHAT   STRONGLY

18. I would write a letter to my Congressman stating my support for programs serving middle class White persons.

DISAGREE   DISAGREE   DISAGREE   AGREE   AGREE   AGREE
STRONGLY   SOMEWHAT   SLIGHTLY   SLIGHTLY   SOMEWHAT   STRONGLY

19. Most middle class White people could take care of themselves if given the opportunity.

DISAGREE   DISAGREE   DISAGREE   AGREE   AGREE   AGREE
STRONGLY   SOMEWHAT   SLIGHTLY   SLIGHTLY   SOMEWHAT   STRONGLY

20. Middle class White people cannot be trusted.

DISAGREE   DISAGREE   DISAGREE   AGREE   AGREE   AGREE
STRONGLY   SOMEWHAT   SLIGHTLY   SLIGHTLY   SOMEWHAT   STRONGLY

21. You cannot tell what middle class White people are going to do from one minute to the next.

DISAGREE   DISAGREE   DISAGREE   AGREE   AGREE   AGREE
STRONGLY   SOMEWHAT   SLIGHTLY   SLIGHTLY   SOMEWHAT   STRONGLY

22. I would not be frightened to have a facility for middle class White people located near my home.

DISAGREE   DISAGREE   DISAGREE   AGREE   AGREE   AGREE
STRONGLY   SOMEWHAT   SLIGHTLY   SLIGHTLY   SOMEWHAT   STRONGLY

23. Middle class White students are responsible for doing poorly in school.

DISAGREE   DISAGREE   DISAGREE   AGREE   AGREE   AGREE
STRONGLY   SOMEWHAT   SLIGHTLY   SLIGHTLY   SOMEWHAT   STRONGLY

24. Middle class White people are more likely to commit violent crimes than other people.

DISAGREE   DISAGREE   DISAGREE   AGREE   AGREE   AGREE
STRONGLY   SOMEWHAT   SLIGHTLY   SLIGHTLY   SOMEWHAT   STRONGLY

25. I would be willing to volunteer some time tutoring a middle class White student.

| DISAGREE | DISAGREE | DISAGREE | AGREE | AGREE | AGREE |
| STRONGLY | SOMEWHAT | SLIGHTLY | SLIGHTLY | SOMEWHAT | STRONGLY |

26. Middle class White people are resistant to the help offered to them.

| DISAGREE | DISAGREE | DISAGREE | AGREE | AGREE | AGREE |
| STRONGLY | SOMEWHAT | SLIGHTLY | SLIGHTLY | SOMEWHAT | STRONGLY |

27. I would be willing to pay more in taxes in order to help middle class White people.

| DISAGREE | DISAGREE | DISAGREE | AGREE | AGREE | AGREE |
| STRONGLY | SOMEWHAT | SLIGHTLY | SLIGHTLY | SOMEWHAT | STRONGLY |

28. Most people are afraid of middle class White people.

| DISAGREE | DISAGREE | DISAGREE | AGREE | AGREE | AGREE |
| STRONGLY | SOMEWHAT | SLIGHTLY | SLIGHTLY | SOMEWHAT | STRONGLY |

ATTITUDE AND BELIEF SCALE VI

Directions:

First write the information about yourself below. Then turn the page.

_____ Male _____Female

Grade_____ Age_____ Birthdate_____

School_____

Ethnicity_____

Have you ever been homeless?	___Y	___N
Has a member of your family ever been homeless?	___Y	___N

Who?_____

Do you know anyone who has ever been homeless?	___Y	___N

Who?_____

Do your parents own the home in which you live?	___Y	___N
Do your parents rent the home in which you live?	___Y	___N

Read each statement and indicate with a circle the degree to which you agree or disagree with the statement.

1. Most middle class Black students require close supervision.

| DISAGREE | DISAGREE | DISAGREE | AGREE | AGREE | AGREE |
| STRONGLY | SOMEWHAT | SLIGHTLY | SLIGHTLY | SOMEWHAT | STRONGLY |

2. Middle class Black students try to manipulate their helpers.

| DISAGREE | DISAGREE | DISAGREE | AGREE | AGREE | AGREE |
| STRONGLY | SOMEWHAT | SLIGHTLY | SLIGHTLY | SOMEWHAT | STRONGLY |

3. Middle class Black students are more dangerous than other people.

| DISAGREE | DISAGREE | DISAGREE | AGREE | AGREE | AGREE |
| STRONGLY | SOMEWHAT | SLIGHTLY | SLIGHTLY | SOMEWHAT | STRONGLY |

4. Middle class Black students do poorly in school.

| DISAGREE | DISAGREE | DISAGREE | AGREE | AGREE | AGREE |
| STRONGLY | SOMEWHAT | SLIGHTLY | SLIGHTLY | SOMEWHAT | STRONGLY |

5. Many Black people are poor because they lost their homes by eviction or foreclosure.

| DISAGREE | DISAGREE | DISAGREE | AGREE | AGREE | AGREE |
| STRONGLY | SOMEWHAT | SLIGHTLY | SLIGHTLY | SOMEWHAT | STRONGLY |

6. I cross the street to avoid middle class Black people.

| DISAGREE | DISAGREE | DISAGREE | AGREE | AGREE | AGREE |
| STRONGLY | SOMEWHAT | SLIGHTLY | SLIGHTLY | SOMEWHAT | STRONGLY |

7. Middle class Black students listen to their teachers.

DISAGREE   DISAGREE   DISAGREE   AGREE   AGREE   AGREE
STRONGLY   SOMEWHAT   SLIGHTLY   SLIGHTLY   SOMEWHAT   STRONGLY

8. It is unsafe to allow middle class Black people to gather in public places.

DISAGREE   DISAGREE   DISAGREE   AGREE   AGREE   AGREE
STRONGLY   SOMEWHAT   SLIGHTLY   SLIGHTLY   SOMEWHAT   STRONGLY

9. The more middle class Black people there are in a neighborhood, the more dangerous that neighborhood becomes.

DISAGREE   DISAGREE   DISAGREE   AGREE   AGREE   AGREE
STRONGLY   SOMEWHAT   SLIGHTLY   SLIGHTLY   SOMEWHAT   STRONGLY

10. Being middle class is largely the result of our economic system.

DISAGREE   DISAGREE   DISAGREE   AGREE   AGREE   AGREE
STRONGLY   SOMEWHAT   SLIGHTLY   SLIGHTLY   SOMEWHAT   STRONGLY

11. Society and government are more responsible for more poverty than middle class Black people.

DISAGREE   DISAGREE   DISAGREE   AGREE   AGREE   AGREE
STRONGLY   SOMEWHAT   SLIGHTLY   SLIGHTLY   SOMEWHAT   STRONGLY

12. I would not be willing to work on a group project in school with a middle class Black student.

DISAGREE   DISAGREE   DISAGREE   AGREE   AGREE   AGREE
STRONGLY   SOMEWHAT   SLIGHTLY   SLIGHTLY   SOMEWHAT   STRONGLY

13. If middle class Black people learn appropriate skills, they could improve their situation.

DISAGREE   DISAGREE   DISAGREE   AGREE   AGREE   AGREE
STRONGLY   SOMEWHAT   SLIGHTLY   SLIGHTLY   SOMEWHAT   STRONGLY

14. Middle class Black students are responsible enough to do their homework and study for tests.

DISAGREE   DISAGREE   DISAGREE   AGREE   AGREE   AGREE
STRONGLY   SOMEWHAT   SLIGHTLY   SLIGHTLY   SOMEWHAT   STRONGLY

15. Middle class Black students are motivated to do well in school.

DISAGREE   DISAGREE   DISAGREE   AGREE   AGREE   AGREE
STRONGLY   SOMEWHAT   SLIGHTLY   SLIGHTLY   SOMEWHAT   STRONGLY

16. Most middle class Black people have chosen to be middle class.

DISAGREE   DISAGREE   DISAGREE   AGREE   AGREE   AGREE
STRONGLY   SOMEWHAT   SLIGHTLY   SLIGHTLY   SOMEWHAT   STRONGLY

17. Even if middle class Black people behave well, it is dangerous to forget that they are middle class.

DISAGREE   DISAGREE   DISAGREE   AGREE   AGREE   AGREE
STRONGLY   SOMEWHAT   SLIGHTLY   SLIGHTLY   SOMEWHAT   STRONGLY

18. I would write a letter to my Congressman stating my support for programs serving middle class Black persons.

DISAGREE   DISAGREE   DISAGREE   AGREE   AGREE   AGREE
STRONGLY   SOMEWHAT   SLIGHTLY   SLIGHTLY   SOMEWHAT   STRONGLY

19. Most middle class Black people could take care of themselves if given the opportunity.

DISAGREE	DISAGREE	DISAGREE	AGREE	AGREE	AGREE
STRONGLY	SOMEWHAT	SLIGHTLY	SLIGHTLY	SOMEWHAT	STRONGLY

20. Middle class Black people cannot be trusted.

DISAGREE	DISAGREE	DISAGREE	AGREE	AGREE	AGREE
STRONGLY	SOMEWHAT	SLIGHTLY	SLIGHTLY	SOMEWHAT	STRONGLY

21. You cannot tell what middle class Black people are going to do from one minute to the next.

DISAGREE	DISAGREE	DISAGREE	AGREE	AGREE	AGREE
STRONGLY	SOMEWHAT	SLIGHTLY	SLIGHTLY	SOMEWHAT	STRONGLY

22. I would not be frightened to have a facility for middle class Black people located near my home.

DISAGREE	DISAGREE	DISAGREE	AGREE	AGREE	AGREE
STRONGLY	SOMEWHAT	SLIGHTLY	SLIGHTLY	SOMEWHAT	STRONGLY

23. Middle class Black students are responsible for doing poorly in school.

DISAGREE	DISAGREE	DISAGREE	AGREE	AGREE	AGREE
STRONGLY	SOMEWHAT	SLIGHTLY	SLIGHTLY	SOMEWHAT	STRONGLY

24. Middle class Black people are more likely to commit violent crimes than other people.

DISAGREE	DISAGREE	DISAGREE	AGREE	AGREE	AGREE
STRONGLY	SOMEWHAT	SLIGHTLY	SLIGHTLY	SOMEWHAT	STRONGLY

25. I would be willing to volunteer some time tutoring a middle class Black student.

DISAGREE	DISAGREE	DISAGREE	AGREE	AGREE	AGREE
STRONGLY	SOMEWHAT	SLIGHTLY	SLIGHTLY	SOMEWHAT	STRONGLY

26. Middle class Black people are resistant to the help offered to them.

DISAGREE	DISAGREE	DISAGREE	AGREE	AGREE	AGREE
STRONGLY	SOMEWHAT	SLIGHTLY	SLIGHTLY	SOMEWHAT	STRONGLY

27. I would be willing to pay more in taxes in order to help middle class Black people.

DISAGREE	DISAGREE	DISAGREE	AGREE	AGREE	AGREE
STRONGLY	SOMEWHAT	SLIGHTLY	SLIGHTLY	SOMEWHAT	STRONGLY

28. Most people are afraid of middle class Black people.

DISAGREE	DISAGREE	DISAGREE	AGREE	AGREE	AGREE
STRONGLY	SOMEWHAT	SLIGHTLY	SLIGHTLY	SOMEWHAT	STRONGLY

Appendix B

SOCIAL DISTANCE SCALE

Write *yes* or *no* in each of the spaces following the name of each group according to whether you would be willing or unwilling to have a member of that group become associated with you in the way indicated.

	BEST FRIEND	FRIEND	PLAYMATE	CLASSMATE	SCHOOL MATE
Black Homeless					
Black Poor, Not Homeless					
Black Not Homeless					
White Homeless					
White Poor, Not Homeless					
White Not Homeless					

Appendix C

SEMANTIC DIFFERENTIAL SCALE I

Directions: Using what you know and the way you feel about White homeless people, please rate White homeless people on the scale below. Place a check mark in the position indicating the direction and intensity of your feeling toward these people. Please take the time to treat each adjective pair as a separate question. Thank you very much.

good	___.___.___.___.___ ___.___.	bad
ugly	___.___.___.___.___.___.___.	beautiful
sweet	___.___.___.___.___.___.___.	sour
clean	___.___.___.___.___.___.___.	dirty
worthless	___.___.___.___.___.___.___.	valuable
cruel	___.___.___.___.___.___.___.	kind
happy	___.___.___.___.___.___.___.	sad
profane	___.___.___.___.___.___.___.	sacred
awful	___.___.___.___.___.___.___.	nice
dishonest	___.___.___.___.___.___.___.	honest
fair	___.___.___.___.___.___.___.	unfair
disreputable	___.___.___.___.___.___.___.	reputable
negative	___.___.___.___.___.___.___.	positive
intelligent	___.___.___.___.___.___.___.	unintelligent
grateful	___.___.___.___.___.___.___.	ungrateful
quarrelsome	___.___.___.___.___.___.___.	congenial
good student	___.___.___.___.___.___.___.	bad student
popular	___.___.___.___.___.___.___.	unpopular
likable	___.___.___.___.___.___.___.	not likable
cooperative	___.___.___.___.___.___.___.	stubborn
unfriendly	___.___.___.___.___.___.___.	friendly

SEMANTIC DIFFERENTIAL SCALE II

Directions: Using what you know and the way you feel about Black homeless people, please rate Black homeless people on the scale below. Place a check mark in the position indicating the direction and intensity of your feeling toward these people. Please take the time to treat each adjective pair as a separate question. Thank you very much.

good	___ . ___ . ___ . ___ . ___ . ___ . ___ .	bad
ugly	___ . ___ . ___ . ___ . ___ . ___ . ___ .	beautiful
sweet	___ . ___ . ___ . ___ . ___ . ___ . ___ .	sour
clean	___ . ___ . ___ . ___ . ___ . ___ . ___ .	dirty
worthless	___ . ___ . ___ . ___ . ___ . ___ . ___ .	valuable
cruel	___ . ___ . ___ . ___ . ___ . ___ . ___ .	kind
happy	___ . ___ . ___ . ___ . ___ . ___ . ___ .	sad
profane	___ . ___ . ___ . ___ . ___ . ___ . ___ .	sacred
awful	___ . ___ . ___ . ___ . ___ . ___ . ___ .	nice
dishonest	___ . ___ . ___ . ___ . ___ . ___ . ___ .	honest
fair	___ . ___ . ___ . ___ . ___ . ___ . ___ .	unfair
disreputable	___ . ___ . ___ . ___ . ___ . ___ . ___ .	reputable
negative	___ . ___ . ___ . ___ . ___ . ___ . ___ .	positive
intelligent	___ . ___ . ___ . ___ . ___ . ___ . ___ .	unintelligent
grateful	___ . ___ . ___ . ___ . ___ . ___ . ___ .	ungrateful
quarrelsome	___ . ___ . ___ . ___ . ___ . ___ . ___ .	congenial
good student	___ . ___ . ___ . ___ . ___ . ___ . ___ .	bad student
popular	___ . ___ . ___ . ___ . ___ . ___ . ___ .	unpopular
likable	___ . ___ . ___ . ___ . ___ . ___ . ___ .	not likable
cooperative	___ . ___ . ___ . ___ . ___ . ___ . ___ .	stubborn
unfriendly	___ . ___ . ___ . ___ . ___ . ___ . ___ .	friendly

SEMANTIC DIFFERENTIAL SCALE III

Directions: Using what you know and the way you feel about poor White people, please rate poor White people on the scale below. Place a check mark in the position indicating the direction and intensity of your feeling toward these people. Please take the time to treat each adjective pair as a separate question. Thank you very much.

good	___.___.___.___.___.___.___.	bad
ugly	___.___.___.___.___.___.___.	beautiful
sweet	___.___.___.___.___.___.___.	sour
clean	___.___.___.___.___.___.___.	dirty
worthless	___.___.___.___.___.___.___.	valuable
cruel	___.___.___.___.___.___.___.	kind
happy	___.___.___.___.___.___.___.	sad
profane	___.___.___.___.___.___.___.	sacred
awful	___.___.___.___.___.___.___.	nice
dishonest	___.___.___.___.___.___.___.	honest
fair	___.___.___.___.___.___.___.	unfair
disreputable	___.___.___.___.___.___.___.	reputable
negative	___.___.___.___.___.___.___.	positive
intelligent	___.___.___.___.___.___.___.	unintelligent
grateful	___.___.___.___.___.___.___.	ungrateful
quarrelsome	___.___.___.___.___.___.___.	congenial
good student	___.___.___.___.___.___.___.	bad student
popular	___.___.___.___.___.___.___.	unpopular
likable	___.___.___.___.___.___.___.	not likable
cooperative	___.___.___.___.___.___.___.	stubborn
unfriendly	___.___.___.___.___.___.___.	friendly

SEMANTIC DIFFERENTIAL SCALE IV

Directions: Using what you know and the way you feel about poor Black people, please rate poor Black people on the scale below. Place a check mark in the position indicating the direction and intensity of your feeling toward these people. Please take the time to treat each adjective pair as a separate question. Thank you very much.

good	___.___.___.___.___.___.___.	bad
ugly	___.___.___.___.___.___.___.	beautiful
sweet	___.___.___.___.___.___.___.	sour
clean	___.___.___.___.___.___.___.	dirty
worthless	___.___.___.___.___.___.___.	valuable
cruel	___.___.___.___.___.___.___.	kind
happy	___.___.___.___.___.___.___.	sad
profane	___.___.___.___.___.___.___.	sacred
awful	___.___.___.___.___.___.___.	nice
dishonest	___.___.___.___.___.___.___.	honest
fair	___.___.___.___.___.___.___.	unfair
disreputable	___.___.___.___.___.___.___.	reputable
negative	___.___.___.___.___.___.___.	positive
intelligent	___.___.___.___.___.___.___.	unintelligent
grateful	___.___.___.___.___.___.___.	ungrateful
quarrelsome	___.___.___.___.___.___.___.	congenial
good student	___.___.___.___.___.___.___.	bad student
popular	___.___.___.___.___.___.___.	unpopular
likable	___.___.___.___.___.___.___.	not likable
cooperative	___.___.___.___.___.___.___.	stubborn
unfriendly	___.___.___.___.___.___.___.	friendly

SEMANTIC DIFFERENTIAL SCALE V

Directions: Using what you know and the way you feel about middle class, White people, please rate middle class, White people on the scale below. Place a check mark in the position indicating the direction and intensity of your feeling toward these people. Please take the time to treat each adjective pair as a separate question. Thank you very much.

good	___. ___. ___. ___. ___. ___. ___. bad
ugly	___. ___. ___. ___. ___. ___. ___. beautiful
sweet	___. ___. ___. ___. ___. ___. ___. sour
clean	___. ___. ___. ___. ___. ___. ___. dirty
worthless	___. ___. ___. ___. ___. ___. ___. valuable
cruel	___. ___. ___. ___. ___. ___. ___. kind
happy	___. ___. ___. ___. ___. ___. ___. sad
profane	___. ___. ___. ___. ___. ___. ___. sacred
awful	___. ___. ___. ___. ___. ___. ___. nice
dishonest	___. ___. ___. ___. ___. ___. ___. honest
fair	___. ___. ___. ___. ___. ___. ___. unfair
disreputable	___. ___. ___. ___. ___. ___. ___. reputable
negative	___. ___. ___. ___. ___. ___. ___. positive
intelligent	___. ___. ___. ___. ___. ___. ___. unintelligent
grateful	___. ___. ___. ___. ___. ___. ___. ungrateful
quarrelsome	___. ___. ___. ___. ___. ___. ___. congenial
good student	___. ___. ___. ___. ___. ___. ___. bad student
popular	___. ___. ___. ___. ___. ___. ___. unpopular
likable	___. ___. ___. ___. ___. ___. ___. not likable
cooperative	___. ___. ___. ___. ___. ___. ___. stubborn
unfriendly	___. ___. ___. ___. ___. ___. ___. friendly

SEMANTIC DIFFERENTIAL SCALE VI

Directions: Using what you know and the way you feel about middle class, Black people, please rate middle class, Black people on the scale below. Place a check mark in the position indicating the direction and intensity of your feeling toward these people. Please take the time to treat each adjective pair as a separate question. Thank you very much.

good	___.___.___.___.___.___.___	bad
ugly	___.___.___.___.___.___.___	beautiful
sweet	___.___.___.___.___.___.___	sour
clean	___.___.___.___.___.___.___	dirty
worthless	___.___.___.___.___.___.___	valuable
cruel	___.___.___.___.___.___.___	kind
happy	___.___.___.___.___.___.___	sad
profane	___.___.___.___.___.___.___	sacred
awful	___.___.___.___.___.___.___	nice
dishonest	___.___.___.___.___.___.___	honest
fair	___.___.___.___.___.___.___	unfair
disreputable	___.___.___.___.___.___.___	reputable
negative	___.___.___.___.___.___.___	positive
intelligent	___.___.___.___.___.___.___	unintelligent
grateful	___.___.___.___.___.___.___	ungrateful
quarrelsome	___.___.___.___.___.___.___	congenial
good student	___.___.___.___.___.___.___	bad student
popular	___.___.___.___.___.___.___	unpopular
likable	___.___.___.___.___.___.___	not likable
cooperative	___.___.___.___.___.___.___	stubborn
unfriendly	___.___.___.___.___.___.___	friendly

Appendix D

INFORMED CONSENT FORM

This form is an agreement between the student, or his/her parent if under 18 years of age, and the investigator. It is designed to inform you of all features of the present study that may reasonably be expected to influence your willingness to participate, provide you with a general understanding of the research procedures, and guarantee your individual rights (or that of your child's) as a research participant throughout the experiment.

This is a study of your (or your child's) attitudes toward various people. You (or your child) will be asked to anonymously answer a questionnaire. When the study is completed, the results will be shared with you at no expense.

There are no risks involved in this study. Please take note of the following:

1.	The investigator is Lawrence Gibel, Ph.D.from Hofstra University, Hempstead, New York 11550. He can be reached through Hofstra's Psychology Department at (516) 463-5624.

2.	You (or your child) may decline to participate in the study or withdraw from the study at any time you wish.

3.	You (or your child) have the right to request that all of your recorded responses be destroyed.

4.	You (and your child) have the right can be sure that the investigator will maintain your confidentiality and anonymity.

5.	A clarification session will follow the experimental procedures. This session will outline the complete nature of the study and answer any questions that you (or your child) may have.

I, _____, have read the above statements and understand their content. My signature below represents my agreement to participate in the above stated study (or have my child participate in the above stated study).

Signed_____ Dated _____

Appendix E

Pearson Correlation Matrix for Demographic Data and Test Scores (n=158)

	Age	Grade	Family Homeless	Know Homeless	Own Home	Rent Home
Age						
Grade	.9436**					
Family HL	.0545	.0069				
Know HL	.0839	.0590	.5075			
Own Home	.1257	.1202	.0595	-.0185		
Rent Home	-.1257	-.1202	-.0595	.0185	-1.0000	
ABS Score	-.0156	-.0098	.0000	.0173	-.0942	.0942
Semantic	-.0217	.0041	-.0088	-.0053	-.0320	.0320
SDI BNPH	.0816	.0663	-.0389	-.0183	.0226	-.0226
SDI BP	.0775	.0587	.0045	.0024	.0065	-.0065
SDI BHL	.1533	.1111	.0167	.0499	-.0088	.0088
SDI WNPH	.0494	.0754	-.0929	-.0598	.0970	-.0970
SDI WP	.0180	.0410	-.0429	-.0074	.0098	-.0098
SDI WHL	.1353	.0922	-.0173	.0644	.0285	-.0285

	ABS	Semantic	SDI BNPH	SDI BP	SDI BH	SDI WNPH
Age	-.0156	-.0217	.0816	.0775	.1533	.0494
Grade	-.0098	.0041	.0663	.0587	.1111	.0754
Family HL	.0000	-.0088	-.0389	.0045	.0167	-.0929
Know HL	.0173	-.0053	-.0183	.0024	.0499	-.0598
Own Home	-.0942	-.0320	.0226	.0065	-.0088	.0970
Rent Home	.0942	.0320	-.0226	-.0065	.0088	-.0970
ABS Score						
SemD	.6702**					
SDI BNPH	-.3676**	-.2953**				
SDI BP	-.3605**	-.2892**	.8020**			
SDI BHL	-.4140**	-.3480**	.6202**	.7563**		
SDI WNPH	-.1103	-.0223	.6287**	.4745**	.2922**	
SDI WP	-.1557	-.0819	.5871**	.7728**	.6013**	.5913**
SDI WHL	-.2341**	-.2355**	.4893**	.6564**	.8234**	.3685**

Appendix E (continued)

Correlations Matrix for Demographic Data and Test Scores

	SDI WP	SDI WHL
Age	.0180	.1353
Grade	.0410	.0922
Family HL	-.0429	-.0173
Know HL	-.0074	.0644
Own Home	.0098	.0285
Rent Home	-.0098	-.0285
ABS Score	-.1557	-.2341**
SemD	-.0819	-.3255**
SDI BNPH	.5871**	.4893**
SDI BP	.7728**	.6564**
SDI BHL	.6013**	.8234**
SDI WNPH	.5913**	.3685**
SDI WP		
SDI WHL	.6793**	

Note. *p ≤ .01, **p ≤ .001

ABS	=	Attitude and Belief Scale
SemD	=	Semantic Differential Scale
SDI	=	Social Distance Scale Interval Data
BNPH	=	Black Nonpoor Housed
BP	=	Black Poor
BHL	=	Black Homeless
WNPH	=	White Nonpoor Housed
WP	=	White Poor
WHL	=	White Homeless

Appendix F

Spearman Correlation Matrix for Demographic Data and Social Distance Scale Guttman (SDG) Data Scores (n=158)

	Age	Grade	Family Homeless	Know Homeless	Own Home	Rent Home
SDG BNPH	.0875	.0589	-.0158	-.0041	.0183	-.0183
SDG BP	.0552	.0323	.0296	.0289	.0047	-.0047
SDG BHL	.1561	.1180	.0463	.0821	-.0027	.0027
SDG WNPH	.0494	.0754	-.0929	-.0598	.0970	-.0970
SDG WP	.0180	.0410	-.0429	-.0074	.0098	-.0098
SDG WHL	.1353	.0922	-.0173	.0644	.0285	-.0285

	ABS	SemD	SDG BNPH	SDG BP	SDG BHL	SDG WNPH
SDG BNPH	-.3776**	-.2897**				
SDG BP	-.3827**	-.2993**	.7750**			
SDG BHL	-.4336**	-.3504**	.5839**	.7399**		
SDG WNPH	-.1103	-.0223	.5973**	.4403**	.2629**	
SDG WP	-.1557	-.0819	.5532**	.7514**	.6052**	.5501**
SDG WHL	-.2341**	-.2355*	.4728**	.6232**	.8362**	.3181**

Appendix F (continued)

Spearman Correlation Matrix for Demographic Data and
Social Distance Scale Gutman (SDG) Data Scores

	SDG WP	SDG WHL
SDG BNPH	.5532**	.4728**
SDG BP	.7514**	.6232**
SDG BHL	.6052**	.8362**
SDG WNPH	.5501**	.3181**
SDG WP		
SDG WHL	.6655**	

Note. *p ≤ .01, **p ≤ .001

ABS	=	Attitude and Belief Scale
SemD	=	Semantic Differential Scale
SDG	=	Social Distance Scale Guttman Data
BNPH	=	Black Nonpoor Housed
BP	=	Black Poor
BHL	=	Black Homeless
WNPH	=	White Nonpoor Housed
WP	=	White Poor
WHL	=	White Homeless

Appendix G

Mean Comparison Tests of Significance for Social Distance Scale Guttman Rank Order Data

Comparison			t	df	p^a
NPH	vs.	PH	8.15	157	<.001
NPH	vs.	HL	14.28	157	<.001
PH	vs.	HL	10.68	157	<.001
WNPH	vs.	BNPH	5.55	157	<.001
WPH	vs.	BPH	9.67	157	<.001
WHL	vs.	BHL	4.20	157	<.001

Note. Modified Bonferroni adjusted alpha for .01, p<.008

[a] Two tailed.

Appendix H

Social Distance Scale Guttman Rank Order Data Mean Scores
and Standard Deviations

| | | TYPE OF PEER | | | |
		Nonpoor Housed	Poor Housed	Homeless	Total
ETHNICITY OF PEER	Black	2.466 (.83)	2.092 (.95)	1.529 (1.02)	2.029 (.93)
	White	2.762 (.59)	2.333 (.92)	1.727 (1.04)	2.274 (.85)
	Total	2.614 (.71)	2.213 (.94)	1.628 (1.03)	2.152 (.89)

Note. Numbers in parentheses are Standard Deviations

Higher scores indicate a more negative attitude

Appendix I

Frequency Distribution of Scores on the ABS

	BNPH	BPH	BHL	WNPH	WPH	WHL
	(n=29)	(n=26)	(n=29)	(n=25)	(n=26)	(n=25)
35-40	x		x		x	
40-45		x			x	
45-50	xxxx	x		xxx	xxx	x
50-55	xxx		xx	xxx	xxxx	x
55-60	xxxxx	x	xxxx	xxxxxxxxxxxx	x	xxx
60-65	x	xxxxxx	xxx	x	xxxx	xxxx
65-70	xxx	xxx	xxx	x	xx	xxx
70-75	xx	xxxx	xx	x	xxxxx	
75-80	xx	xxx	x	x	xxx	xx
80-85	xx	x		xx		xxxx
85-90	x	xxxx	xxx	x		xxxx
90-95	xx	xx	x		x	
95-100	xx	x	xx		x	x
100-105			xxx			x
105-110			xx			
110-115						
115-120	x					x
120-125						
125-130						
130-135						
135-140						
140-145						
145-150						
155-160			x			

Note. x = one score.

BNPH = Black nonpoor housed.
BPH   = Black poor housed.
BHL   = Black homeless.
WNPH = White nonpoor housed.
WPH   = White poor housed.
WHL   = White homeless.

Appendix J

Frequency Distribution of Scores on the SemD

	BNPH	BPH	BHL	WNPH	WPH	WHL
	(n=27)	(n=26)	(n=28)	(n=25)	(n=26)	(n=25)
25-30				x		
30-35		x				
35-40	xx					
40-45	x	x		x		
45-50			x	xxx		
50-55	xx	xx	x	xx		
55-60	xx			xxxx	x	
60-65	xxx		x	xxx	xx	
65-70				xx	x	x
70-75		xx	x	x	xxxx	xx
75-80	xxxx	xxxxxx	xxx	xxxxxx	xxx	xxxx
80-85	xxx	xxxx	xxx	x	xxxxx	xxxxxxx
85-90	xxx	xxxxx	xxxx		xx	xxxx
90-95	xxx	xx	x	x	xxxx	
95-100	xx	x	xxx		x	xx
100-105	xx		xxx			x
105-110		xx	xxx		xx	x
110-115			x		x	
115-120			x			
120-125			xx			xx
125-130						
130-135						
135-140						x

Note. x = one score.

BNPH = Black nonpoor housed.
BPH = Black poor housed.
BHL = Black homeless.
WNPH = White nonpoor housed.
WPH = White poor housed.
WHL = White homeless.

Appendix K

Cochran's C Test for Homogenity of Variance for the Attitude and Belief Scale (ABS) and Semantic Differential Scale (SemD) (n=158)

Data Source	Comparison	C	p
ABS	Race	.63	.020
ABS	SES	.47	.018
SemD	Race	.58	.150
SemD	SES	.37	.760

References

Adorno, T. W., Levinson, D. J., Frenkel-Brunswik, E., & Sanford, R. N. (1950). *The authoritarian personality.* New York: Harper.

Apetekar, L. (1990). "How ethnic differences within a culture influence child rearing: The case of Columbian street children." *Journal of Comparative Family Studies, 21,* 67-79.

Alperstein, G., Rappaport, C., & Flanagan, J. M. (1988). "Health problems of homeless children in New York City." *American Journal of Public Health, 78,* 1232-1233.

Barney, J. A., Fredericks, J., Fredericks, M., & Robinson, P. (1985). "Business students and social awareness: A study of business students' attitudes." *Journal of Instructional Psychology, 12,* 152-158.

Bassuk, E. L. (1984). "The homeless problem." *Scientific American, 251,* 40-45.

Bassuk, E. L. (1987). "The feminization of homelessness: Families in Boston shelters." *American Journal of Social Psychiatry, 7,* 19-23.

Bassuk, E. L., & Gallagher, E. M. (1990). "The impact of homelessness on children." *Child and Youth Services, 14,* 19-33.

Bassuk, E. L., & Rosenberg, L. (1988). "Why does family homelessness occur? A case-control study." *American Journal of Public Health, 78,* 783-88.

Bassuk, E. L., & Rubin, L. (1987). "Homeless children: A neglected population." *American Journal of Orthopsychiatry, 57,* 279-286.

Bassuk, E. L., Rubin, L., & Lauriet, A. S. (1986). " Characteristics of sheltered homeless families." *American Journal of Public Health, 76,* 1097-1101.

Baxter, E., & Hopper, K. (1981). *Private lives/public spaces: Homeless adults on the streets of New York City.* New York: Community Service Society of New York.

Belcher, J. R., & DiBlasio, F. A. (1990). "The needs of depressed homeless persons: Designing appropriate services." *Community Mental Health Journal, 26,* 355-266.

Bellows, R. (1961). *Psychology of personnel in business and industry.* Englewood Cliffs, NJ: Prentice-Hall.

Benjamin, S. E. (1989). "Color blind? The influence of race on perception of crime severity." *Journal of Negro Education, 58,* 442-448.

Bogardus, E. S. (1925). Measuring social distances. *Journal of Applied Sociology, 9,* 299-308.

Bogardus, E. S. (1933). "A social distance scale." *Sociology and Social Research, 17,* 265-271.

Bogardus, E. S. (1937). "Social distance and its practical implications." *Sociology and Social Research, 22*, 462-476.

Bogardus, E. S. (1939). "Scales in social research." *Sociology and Social Research, 24*, 69-75.

Bretzing, B. H. & Caterino, L. C. (1984). "Group counseling with elementary students. Special Issue: Computers in school psychology." *School Psychology Review, 13*, 515-518.

Buros, O. K. (1970). *Personality tests and reviews.* Highland Park, NJ: Gryphon Press.

Byrnes, D. A. (1988). "Children and prejudice." *Social Education, 52*, 267-271.

Carling, P. J. (1990). "Major mental illness, housing and supports." *American Psychologist, 45*, 969-975.

Carter, R. (1990). "The relationship between racism and racial identity among White Americans: An exploratory study." *Journal of Counseling and Development, 69*, 46-50.

Catholic Charities, Diocese of Metuchen. (1991). *Statistics FY '90.* (Services fact sheet prepared by Catholic Charities). Metuchen, NJ: Author.

Chafel, J. A. (1990). "Children in poverty: Policy perspectives on a national crisis." *Young Children, 45*(5), 31-37.

Claney, D., & Parker, W. M. (1989). "Assessing White racial consciousness and perceived comfort with Black individuals: A preliminary study." *Journal of Counseling and Development, 67*, 449-451.

Congress of the United States, Washington, DC, House Committee on Ways and Means. (1988). *Use of AFDC funds for homeless families.* Joint hearing before the Subcommittee on Public Assistance and Unemployment comprised of the Committee on Ways and Means, House of Representatives and the Subcommittee on Social Security and Family Policy of the Committee on Finance, United States Senate.

Congress of the United States, Washington, DC, House Select Committee on Children, Youth and Families. (1989). Working families at the margins: The uncertain future of America's small towns. *Hearing before the Select Committee on Children, Youth and Families.* House of Representatives. 101st Congress 1st Session.

Daly, G. (1990). "Health implications of homelessness: Reports from three countries." *Journal of Sociology and Social Welfare, 17*, 111-125.

Damico, S. B., Bell-Nathaniel, A., & Green, C. (1981). "Effects of school organizational structure on interracial friendships in middle schools." *Journal of Educational Research, 74*, 388-393.

Davidson, B. P., & Jenkins, P. J. (1989). "Class diversity in shelter life." *Social Work, 34*, 491-495.

Doolan, J., Georgedes, D., Dillman, G., & Willis, I. (1989). *The education of homeless children and youth in New Jersey: A plan for state action.* Trenton, NJ: New Jersey Department of Education.

Dovidio, J. F., Evans, N., & Tyler, R. B. (1986). "Racial stereotypes: The contents of their cognitive representations." *Journal of Experimental Social Psychology, 22,* 22-37.

Dusenbury, L., Botvin, G. J., & James-Ortiz, S. (1989). "The primary prevention of adolescent substance abuse through the promotion of personal and social competence." *Prevention in Human Services, 7,* 201-224.

Eddowes, E., & Hranitz, J. R. (1989). "Educating children of the homeless." *Childhood Education, 65*(4), 197-200.

Edelman, M. W., & Mihaly, L. (1989). "Homeless families and the housing crisis in the United States. Special Issue: Runaway, homeless and shut-out children and youth in Canada, Europe, and the United States." *Children and Youth Services Review, 11,* 91-108.

Ely, L. (1987). *Broken lives: Denial of education to homeless* children. Washington, DC: National Coalition for the Homeless.

Farrell, W. C., & Jones, C. K. (1988). "Recent racial incidents in higher education: A preliminary perspective. Special issue: Racial and ethnic issues in higher education." *Urban Review, 20,* 211-226.

Ferguson, S. (1990). "Us vs. them: America's growing frustration with the homeless." *Pacific New Service* (April 16, 1990). In *Utne Reader, 41,* 50-55.

First, R. J., Roth, D., & Arewa, B. D. (1988). "Homelessness: Understanding the dimensions of the problem for minorities." *Social Work, 33,* 120-124.

First, R. J., Toomey, B. G., & Rife, J. C. (1990). *Preliminary findings on rural homelessness in Ohio.* Columbus, OH: Ohio State University, College of Social Work.

Gagne, J. & Dorvil, H. (1988). "L'itinerance: le regard sociologique [Homelessness: A sociological perspective]." *Revue Quebecoise de Psychologie, 9,* 63-78. (From PsycLIT Database, 1990. Abstract No. 02259885)

General Accounting Office. (1989). *Children and youth: About 68,000 homeless and 186,000 in shared housing at any given time.* (Report to Congressional committees). Washington, DC: Author. (ERIC Document Reproduction Service No. ED 312 076)

Gonzalez, M. L. (1990). "School + home = A program for educating homeless students." *Phi Delta Kappan, 71,* 785-787.

Gore, A. (1990). "Public policy and the homeless." *American Psychologist, 45,* 960-962.

Grant, R. (1990). "The special needs of homeless children: Early interventions at a welfare hotel." *Topics in Early Childhood Special Education, 10,* 76-91.

Gresham, F. M., & Elliot, S. N. (1990). *Social Skills Rating System.* Circle Pines, MN: American Guidance Service.

Grinspoon, L. (Ed.). (1990). "Mental illness and homelessness: Part I." *The Harvard Mental Health Letter, 7,* 1-4.

Grunberg, J., & Eagle, P. F. (1990). "Shelterization: How the homeless adapt to shelter living." *Hospital and Community Psychiatry, 41,* 521-525.

Hagan, J. L. (1987). "Gender and homelessness." *Social Work, 32,* 312-316.

Hartman, A. (1989). "Homelessness: Public issue and private trouble." *Social Work, 34,* 483-484.

Hartup, W. W. (1989). "Social relationships and their developmental significance." *American Psychologist, 44,* 120-126.

Henerson, M. E., Morris, L. L., & Fitz-Gibbon, C. T. (1987). *How to measure attitudes.* Newbury Park, CA: SAGE Publications.

Hickson, J., & Gaydon, V. (1989). "'Twilight children': The street children of Johannesburg." *Journal of Multicultural Counseling and Development, 17,* 85-94.

Hombs, M. E., & Snyder, M. (Eds.). (1986). *Homelessness in America: A forced march to nowhere.* Washington, DC: Community for Creative Non-Violence.

Hopper, K. (1984). "A quiet violence: The homeless poor in New York City, 1982." In M. E. Hombs & M. Snyder (Eds.), *Homelessness in America: A forced march to nowhere* (pp. 61-68). Washington, DC: Community for Creative Non-Violence.

Horowitz, S. V., Springer, C. M., & Kose, G. (1988). "Stress in hotel children: The effects of homelessness on attitudes toward school." *Children's Environments Quarterly, 5,* 31-36.

Hutchison, W. J., Searight, P., & Stretch, J. J. (1986). "Multidimensional networking: A response to the needs of homeless families." *Social Work, 31,* 427-436.

Jacobs, W. R. (1978). "The effect of the learning disability label on classroom teachers ability objectively to observe and interpret child behaviors." *Learning Disabilities Quarterly, 1,* 50-55.

James, W. H., Smith, A. J., & Mann, R. (1991). "Educating Homeless Children." *Childhood Education, 67,* 305-308.

Johnson, A. K. (1989). "Measurement and methodology: Problems and issues in research on homelessness." *Social Work Research and Abstracts, 25,* 12-20.

Johnson, A. K., & Kreuger, L. W. (1989). "Toward a better understanding of homeless women." *Social Work, 34,* 537-540.

Kass, F., & Silver, J. M. (1990). "Neuropsychiatry and the homeless." *Journal of Neuropsychiatry and Clinical Neurosciences, 2,* 15-19.

Keller, C. E., Hallahan, D. P., McShane, E. A., Crowley, E. P., & Blanford, B. J. (1990). "The coverage of persons with disabilities in American newspapers." *The Journal of Special Education, 24,* 271-282.

Keppel, G. (1982). *Design and analysis a researcher's handbook.* Englewood Cliffs, NJ: Prentice-Hall, Inc.

Kidder, L. H., Judd, C. M., & Smith, E. R. (1986). *Research methods in social relations.* New York: Holt, Rinehart and Winston, Inc.

Knapp, M. S., & Shields, P. M. (1990). "Reconceiving academic instruction for children of poverty." *Phi Delta Kappan, 71,* 753-758.

Levine, I. S., & Rog, D. J. (1990). "Mental health services for homeless mentally ill persons." *American Psychologist, 45,* 963-968.

Lindley, A. (1994). *Teacher's attitudes and expectation as a predictor of a homeless student's success in school (school success).* Unpublished doctoral dissertation, Hofstra University, Hempstead, NY.

Linn, L. S., Gelberg, L., & Leake, B. (1990). "Substance abuse and mental health status of homeless and domiciled low-income users of a medical clinic." *Hospital and Community Psychiatry, 41,* 306-310.

Marcus, R. F., Flatter, C., Talabis, P., Ford, C., Conahan, F., & Catoe, R. (1991, April 20). *Homelessness and its impact on child and family functioning.* Paper presented at the Biennial Meeting of the Society for Research in Child Development, Seattle, WA.

Marks, M. (1992). *Beliefs, contact and attitudes towards homeless persons of health care students and practitioners.* Unpublished doctoral dissertation, Hofstra University, Hempstead, NY.

Martagon, M., Ramirez, M., & Masten, A. S. (1991, April). *Future aspirations of homeless children.* Poster presented for the Society for Research In Child Development Conference, Seattle, WA.

Maza, P. L., & Hall, J. A. (1988). *Homeless children and their families: A preliminary study.* Washington, DC: Child Welfare League of America.

McCombs, R. C., & Gay, J. (1988). "Effects of race, class, and IQ information on judgements of parochial grade school teachers." *Journal of Social Psychology, 128,* 647-652.

Mills, C., & Ota, H. (1989). "Homeless women with minor children in the Detroit metropolitan area." *Social Work, 34,* 485-489.

Missouri Department of Elementary & Secondary Education. (1989). *Meeting the educational needs of Missouri's homeless children.* Jefferson City, MO: Author.

Molnar, A. (1989). "Turning children into things. *Educational Leadership, 46(8),* 68-69.

Muir, D. E. (1989). "'White' attitudes toward 'Blacks' at a deep-south university campus, 1963-1988." *Sociology and Social Research, 73* (2), 84-89.

Myers, D. G. (1990). *Social Psychology* (pp. 330-366). NY: McGraw Hill.

National Coalition for the Homeless. (1987a). *Homelessness in the United States: Background and federal response. A briefing paper for Presidential candidates.* Washington, DC: Author. In Rafferty, Y. & Rollins, N. (1989). *Learning in limbo: The educational deprivation of homeless children.* New York: Advocates for Children of New York.

National Coalition for the Homeless. (1987b). *Pushed out: America's homeless. Thanksgiving 1987.* Washington DC: Author.

National Coalition for the Homeless. (1989). *American nightmare: A decade of homelessness in the United States.* Washington DC: Author.

New Jersey Administrative Code. Title 6. Education (1990).

New York State Department of Education. (1988). *Report on the homeless in New York State.* Albany, NY: Author. In Rafferty, Y. & Rollins, N. (1989). *Learning in limbo: The educational deprivation of homeless children.* New York: Advocates for Children of New York.

New York State Education Department, Division of Student Development and Family Support Services. (1989). *The New York State plan for the education of homeless children and youth 1989-1991.* Albany, NY: Author.

Osgood, C. E., Suci, G. J., & Tannenbaum, P. H. (1957). *The measurement of meaning.* Urbana: University of Illinois Press.

Pedhazur, E. J., & Schmelkin, L. P. (1991). *Measurement, design and analysis: An integrated approach.* Hillsdale: Lawrence Erlbaum Associates.

Pine, G. J., & Hilliard III, A. G. (1990). "Rx for racism: Imperatives for America's schools." *Phi Delta Kappan, 71,* 593-600.

Plotnick, R. D. (1989). "Directions for reducing child poverty." *Social Work, 34,* 523-530.

Polakow-Suransky, S., & Ulaby, N. (1990). "Students take action to combat racism." *Phi Delta Kappan, 71,* 601-605.

Rafferty, Y., & Rollins, N. (1989a). *Learning in limbo: The educational deprivation of homeless children.* New York: Advocates for Children of New York.

Rafferty, Y., & Rollins, N. (1989b, August). *The impact of homelessness on children: No time to lose.* Paper presented at the American Psychological Association convention, New Orleans, LA.

Rafferty, Y., & Shinn, M. (1991). "The impact of homelessness on children." *American Psychologist, 46,* 1170-1179.

Rescola, L., Parker, R., & Stolley, P. (1991). "Ability, achievement and adjustment in homeless children." *American Journal of Orthopsychiatry, 61,* 210-221.

Richey, L. P. & Ysseldyke, J. E. (1983). "Teachers' expectations for the younger siblings of learning disabled students." *Journal for Learning Disabilities, 16,* 610-615.

Roseman, M., & Stein, M. L. (1990). "Homeless children: A new vulnerability." *Child and Youth Services, 14,* 89-109.

Rossi, P. H. (1990). "The old homeless and the new homeless in historical perspective." *American Psychologist, 45,* 954-959.

Sager, H. A., & Schofield, J. W. (1980). "Race and gender barriers: Preadolescent peer behavior in academic classrooms." Paper presented at the American Psychological Association convention. In D. G. Myers, (1990). *Social Psychology* (pp. 330-366). NY: McGraw Hill.

Sales, B. (1986). "Rehabilitation psychology and law. Special Issue: Rehabilitation psychology and the law." *Rehabilitation Psychology, 31,* 5-11.

Schofield, J. W. (1982). "Black and white in school: Trust, tension or tolerance?" In D. G. Myers, (1990). *Social Psychology* (pp. 330-366). NY: McGraw Hill.

Schofield, J. W. (1986). "Causes and consequences of the colorblind perspective." In D. G. Myers, (1990). *Social Psychology* (pp. 330-366). NY: McGraw Hill.

Schumack, S. (Ed.). (1987). "The educational rights of homeless children." *Newsnotes, 38.* (ERIC Document Reproduction Service No. ED 288 915)

Searcy, S. (1988). "Developing self-esteem." *Academic Therapy, 23,* 453-460.

Sherman, R. L. (1990). "Intergroup conflict on high school campuses." *Journal of Multicultural Counseling and Development, 18,* 11-18.

Solarz, A., & Bogat, G. A. (1990). "When social support fails: The homeless." *Journal of Community Psychology, 18,* 79-96.

Somerman, F. B. (1990). "Value, attitude and belief determinants of willingness to accept a facility for the homeless (Doctoral dissertation, City University of New York, 1990)." *Dissertation Abstracts International, 51,* 03B.

State of New Jersey Department of Education, Office of Public Information. (1989). *News release: State unveils plan for education of homeless children.* Trenton, NJ: Author.

Staub, E. (1996). "Cultural-societal roots of violence." *American Psychologist, 51,* 117-132.

Stewart B. McKinney Act, Public Law 100-77 Section 103 (1987).

Stewart, C. C. (1988). "Modification of student attitudes toward disabled peers." *Adapted Physical Education Quarterly, 5,* 44-48.

Stronge, J. H., & Tenhouse, C. (1990). *Educating homeless children: Issues and answer.* Bloomington, IN: Phi Delta Kappa Educational Foundation.

Sutherland, J. & Algozzine, B. (1979). "The learning disabled label as a biasing factor in the visual-motor performance of normal children." *Journal of Learning Disabilities, 12,* 17-23.

Thomas, F. F., & Lee, D. (1990). "Effects of ethnicity and physical disability on academic and social ratings of photographs." *Psychological Reports, 67,* 240-242.

Thompson, C. E., Neville, H., Weather, P. L., Poston, W., et al. (1990). "Cultural mistrust and racism reaction among African-American students." *Journal of College Student Development, 31,* 162-168. (From PsycLIT database, 1990, Abstract No. 08975246)

Toro, P. A., & McDonell, D. M. (1992). "Beliefs, attitudes and knowledge about homelessness: A survey of the general public." *American Journal of Community Psychology, 20,* 53-80.

Tower, C. C., & White, D. J. (1989). *Homeless students.* Washington, DC: National Education Association. (ERIC Document Reproduction Service No. ED 311 228).

U. S. Department of Education. (February 15, 1989). *Report to Congress on state interim reports of the education of homeless children.* Walsh, M. E., & Buckley, M. A. (1994). "Children's experiences of homelessness: Implications for school counselors." *Elementary School Guidance and Counseling, 29,* 4-15.

Washington, D.C.: Author. In Rafferty, Y. & Rollins, N. (1989). *Learning in Limbo: The educational deprivation of homeless children.* New York: Advocates for Children of New York.

Whitman, B. Y., Accardo, P., Boyert, M., & Kendagor, R. (1990). "Homelessness and cognitive performance in children: A possible link." *Social Work, 35,* 516-519.

Winborne, D. G., & Murray, G. J. (1992). "Address unknown: An exploration of the educational and social attitudes of homeless adolescents." *High School Journal, 75,* 144-149.

Yuker, H. E. (1987). "Labels can hurt people with disabilities." *Etc., 44,* 16-22.

Zeligs, R. & Hendrickson, G. (1933). "Racial attitudes of two hundred sixth grade children." *Sociology and Social Research, 18,* 26-36.

Zeligs, R. & Hendrickson, G. (1933). "Factors regarded by children as the basis of their racial attitudes." *Sociology and Social Research, 19,* 225-233.

Zeligs, R. (1936). "Racial attitudes of children." *Sociology and Social Research, 21,* 361-371.

Index